That's Funny!

A Compendium of
Over 1,000
Great Jokes
From Today's
Hottest Comedians

CADER BOOKS

Andrews and McMeel
A Universal Press Syndicate Company
Kansas City

THANK YOU for buying this Cader Book—we hope you enjoy it. And thanks as well to the store that sold you this, and the hardworking sales rep who sold it to them. It takes a lot of people to make a book (even a silly one). Here are some of the many who were instrumental:

EDITORIAL: Lisa Jenner Hudson, Genevieve Field, Jake Morrissey, Dorothy O'Brien, Regan Brown
DESIGN: Charles Kreloff, Orit Mardkha-Tenzer
COPY EDITING/PROOFING: Susan Groake, Robert Legault
PRODUCTION: Carole Coe, Cathy Kirkland

© 1996 Cader Company Inc. All rights reserved. No part of this book may be used or reproduced in any manner whatsoever without written permission of the Publisher. Printed in the United States of America.

If you would like to share any thoughts about this book, or are interested in other books by us, please write to:
Cader Books, 38 E. 29th Street, New York, NY, 10016

Or find us at our new web site: http://www.caderbooks.com

Library of Congress Cataloging-in-Publication Number: 96-83770

ISBN: 0-8362-1502-8
May 1996

10 9 8 7 6 5

ATTENTION SCHOOLS AND BUSINESSES:
Andrews and McMeel books are available at quantity discounts with bulk purchase for educational, business, or sales promotional use. For information, please write to: Special Sales Department, Andrews and McMeel, 4520 Main Street, Kansas City, Missouri 64111.

Contents

> *I love being married. I was single for a long time and I just got sick of finishing my own sentences.*
> –BRIAN KILEY

> *Yeah, I saw my parents today.... It's all right, they didn't see me or anything.*
> –MARGARET SMITH

Do you think Clinton would have stayed in D.C. if it had been the Million Woman March?
–WILL DURST

The reason most people play golf is to wear clothes they would not be caught dead in otherwise.
–ROGER SIMON

The trouble with the rat race is that even if you win you are still a rat.
–LILY TOMLIN

It All Started in the Garden...

> *Before I met my husband, I'd never fallen in love—though I've stepped in it a few times.*
> —RITA RUDNER

Dating

I don't think of myself as single. I'm romantically challenged. –STEPHANIE PIRO

My success has allowed me to strike out with a higher class of women. –WOODY ALLEN

While I'm in a wig I'm pretty attractive. I stare at mirrors because I'm my type. –KEVIN MCDONALD

I can't get a relationship to last longer than it takes to make copies of their tapes. –MARGARET SMITH

I think; therefore, I'm single. –LIZZ WINSTEAD

A man on a date wonders if he'll get lucky. The woman already knows. –MONICA PIPER

A woman broke up with me and sent me pictures of her and her new boyfriend in bed together. Solution? I sent them to her dad. –CHRISTOPHER CASE

How many women here like to have sex in the morning? Now how many like to be awake when it happens? –MARSHA WARFIELD

A new cologne is coming out. It's for cowboys and it's made from cow manure. That way the women will be on you like flies. –BILL MAHER

I date this girl for two years—and then the nagging starts: "I wanna know your name." –MIKE BINDER

As long as I've done stand-up, I've talked about dating. Now I'm involved in a relationship 'cause I figured, "Hey, what could be worse than dating?" –GARRY SHANDLING

I like ugly men. *[To the audience]* I know a couple of you feel the same way. –MARSHA WARFIELD

I once dated a guy who was so dumb he could not count to 21 unless he was naked. –JOAN RIVERS

Relationships don't last anymore. When I meet a guy, the first question I ask myself is, "Is this the man I want my children to spend their weekends with?" –RITA RUDNER

I've actually seen a man walk up to four women sitting in a bar and say, "Hey, what are you doing all alone?"
–LILY TOMLIN

Do you know what is the best way for a guy to impress a girl at the gym? The best way is to do pull-ups...pull up in a Corvette, pull up in a Rolls-Royce, pull up in a Cadillac. –CONAN O'BRIEN

Single women used to go out on a beautiful night like this looking for hip, cool guys who look like they know what they are doing. You know what I'm looking for? A file clerk who looks like he hasn't been laid in 15 years. –ELAYNE BOOSLER

I went home to Chicago recently. I'm from the South Side, you know. I ran into some people I had not seen in a long time. I went out with this one guy and he had a few drinks and he started acting weird. I didn't want to ask him if he was mental or anything like that. So I asked him, "Bob, when you went to school, did you ride the short bus or the long bus?" –MARGARET SMITH

I'm looking for a perfume to overpower men—I'm sick of karate. –PHYLLIS DILLER

Love for me has always been like a pretzel. Twisted and salty. –EMMY GAY

I'm very single. I was going with someone for a few years, but we broke up. It was one of those things. He wanted to get married. And I didn't want him to.

–RITA RUDNER

I went out to dinner with a Marine last weekend. He looked across the table and he goes, "I could kill you in seven seconds." I go, "I'll just have toast then." –MARGARET SMITH

Every time a baseball player grabs his crotch, it makes him spit. That's why you should never date a baseball player. –MARSHA WARFIELD

Just 'cause you look at another woman, it doesn't mean you are going to do anything. I mean, you are at a restaurant and food comes to another table, you might look at it. It doesn't mean you are gonna dive in and start eating it. It's not like I look at another woman and turn to my girlfriend and say, "I wish I got that. Why didn't I get what's he's having?" –GARRY SHANDLING

I just broke up with someone. He was a comic. I'm glad we broke up before we were married because can you imagine the custody battle between two divorcing comics? It would be like, "All right, I get the joke about the house. You get the joke about the car." "What about the kids?" "Ahh, take 'em. They're not that funny." –LYNN HARRIS

I just broke up with someone and the last thing she said to me was, "You'll never find anyone like me again!" I'm thinking, "I should hope not! If I don't want you, why would I want someone like you?" –LARRY MILLER

Don't you hate it when you date someone and they say this, "I love you but I'm not in love with you." You just want to go, "I want you, but not inside me." –FELICIA MICHAELS

I'm a nice girl. I hate it on the first date when I accidentally have sex. –EMMY GAY

Guys, you know what the most expensive thing in the world is? A girl that is free for the evening. –SHERYL BERNSTEIN

In high school, my sister went out with the captain of the chess team. My parents loved him because he was the captain of the chess team. They figured that any guy that took hours to make a move was okay with them. –BRIAN KILEY

It's hard to talk to divorced men—always sensitive from the divorce. Take things the wrong way. "Nice day, don't you think?" "I don't want to make a commitment." "Want half of my ice cream?" "I don't want half of anything anymore." –ELAYNE BOOSLER

My Aunt Lorraine said, "Bob, you're gay. Are you seeing a psychiatrist?" I said, "No, I'm seeing a lieutenant in the Navy." –BOB SMITH

I joined a singles group in my neighborhood. The other day the president called me up and said, "Welcome to the group. I want to find out what kind of activities you like to plan." I said, "Well, weddings." –LYNN HARRIS

The whole dating ritual was different when I was a kid. Girls got pinned—not nailed. –BILL MAHER

This guy came up to me at a bar and said, "Hey Cupcake, can I buy you a drink?" I said, "No, but I'll take the three bucks." –MARGARET SMITH

I love to shop after a bad relationship. I don't know. I buy a new outfit and it makes me feel better. It just does. Sometimes if I see a really great outfit, I'll break up with someone on purpose. –RITA RUDNER

The difference between being in a relationship and being in prison is that in prisons they let you play softball on the weekends. –BOBBY KELTON

You can test people before you date them. Have them come to the door. "Hi, ready in a second. Just sewing this button on a jacket. Oops. Pricked your finger? I'll get a slide." –ELAYNE BOOSLER

Relationships are hard. It's like a full-time job, and we should treat it like one. If your boyfriend or girlfriend wants to leave you, they should give you two weeks notice, there should be severance pay, and before they leave, they should have to find you a temp. –BOB ETTINGER

You got to be on your toes when you are reading personal ads. So many of the guys feel the need to point out that they are like Seinfeld. Basically, what that tells me is that they have weird, annoying friends. –LYNN HARRIS

Let's face it, a date is like a job interview that lasts all night. The only difference between the two is that there are very few job interviews where there's a chance you will end up naked at the end of it. –JERRY SEINFELD

A lot of break-up songs have the same theme—the guy sings, "Baby, you're seeing somebody new now and if he treats you bad, I'll always be here for you 'cause I love you very much." Why don't they make that a little more realistic? "You're seeing someone new now, and if he treats you bad, good!" –ADAM SANDLER

I'm very loyal in a relationship. Any relationship. When I go out with my mom, I don't look at other moms. I don't go, "Oooooh, I wonder what her macaroni and cheese tastes like."

–GARRY SHANDLING

I feel if I'm lucky, I'll fall in love. If I'm unlucky, I'll fall and hit my head. –EMMY GAY

Husbands and Wives

My wife's a water sign. I'm an earth sign. Together we make mud. –RODNEY DANGERFIELD

Ah, yes, divorce, from the Latin word meaning to rip out a man's genitals through his wallet. –ROBIN WILLIAMS

What do you do if your wife won't talk to you? Enjoy. –SIMON RAKOFF

We've been trying to have a kid. Well, she was trying. I just laid there. –BOB SAGET

A psychiatrist asks a lot of expensive questions that your wife asks for nothing. –JOEY ADAMS

In temple I kept hearing Jewish men make good husbands. And I'm thinking, "Then who's this guy living in my house?" –BETSY SALKIND

The worst thing to do during a separation is to go through your photo albums. They're just full of great memories: vacations, birthdays, Christmas. I guess that's 'cause we never take photographs of lousy moments we share together. Next time you're having a fight, stop for a snapshot. –BRENT BIASKOSKI

The two times they pronounce you anything in life is when you are man and wife or they pronounce you dead on arrival. –DENNIS MILLER

I was driving and I wanted to buy her [my wife] freeway flowers at the off ramp. They were out of flowers. So I bought her a sack of oranges. She loves me. She put them in a vase. –BOB SAGET

On getting married: You lose the ability to get dressed by yourself. –PAUL REISER

Husbands are like fires. They go out when unattended. –ZSA ZSA GABOR

I was at one wedding and the priest was skeptical. You know that part where he has to say, "If anyone can show why these two people should not be together"? He goes, "Then line up behind the microphone I set up and I'll try to get to as many of you as I can before lunch." –MARK FARRELL

On glasses: My wife made me get them. I wasn't seeing things her way. –MARK KLEIN

Marriage is a give and take. You'd better give it to her or she'll take it away.

–JOEY ADAMS

My cousin just got married for the totally wrong reasons. She married a man for money. She wasn't real subtle about it. Instead of calling him her fiancé, she kept calling him her financee. –RITA RUDNER

I walked in on my wife and the milkman, the first thing she says is, "Don't tell the butcher!" –RODNEY DANGERFIELD

Marrying a man is like buying something you've been admiring for a long time in a shop window. You may love it when you get it home, but it doesn't always go with everything else in the house. –JEAN KERR

A man wins the lottery. He says to his wife, "I've got it made! Start packing." She says, "Am I packing for cold weather or warm?" He says, "How the hell should I know, just be out by the time I get back!" –RED BUTTONS

You ever go to a wedding where you know the marriage isn't going to last? You don't want to say anything, but you don't want to spend a hundred bucks on a gift either. It's a dilemma. "Here's a lottery ticket. Good luck to you." –MARK FARRELL

A man in love is incomplete until he is married. Then he is finished.

–ZSA ZSA GABOR

We had a guy in here last night who thought loading the dishwasher meant getting his wife drunk. –JEFF FOXWORTHY

My husband said he needs more space. So I locked him outside. –ROSEANNE

A psychiatrist told me and my wife we should have sex every night—now we'll never see each other. –RODNEY DANGERFIELD

My fiancée told me the rule of thumb on how much to spend on an engagement ring was two months' salary. So I moved to Haiti for a couple months, made a buck eighty. Nice plywood ring—no knots. I sanded it myself. –BARRY KENNEDY

Once a friend of my ex-husband came up to me and said, "Your ex-husband jokes are mean." I said, "That may be true, but which among his friends has been cruel enough to explain them to him?" –BRETT BUTLER

In August, my husband, Morris, and I celebrated our 38th wedding anniversary. You know what I finally realized? If I had killed the man the first time I thought about it, I'd have been out of jail by now. –ANITA MILNER

Why can't we be honest with wedding invitations and have them printed with a $50 cover, two-drink minimum? –CLAUDIA SHERMAN

My dad came to my wedding day with this advice, "Son, don't ever cheat on your wife. You don't want to risk your life's happiness for eight minutes of pleasure." "You're up to eight minutes?" –MARK KLEIN

After you've been married for a while, the women will start choosing your clothes. If you protest they'll say, "Dressing is a privilege. You abused it and now you've lost it." –CARY LONG

Eventually in your life, you have to get married. You just have to. That's probably what I'll say at the ceremony. I'll go, "I have to." –GARRY SHANDLING

They should replace the *Wedding March* with the theme from *Mission Impossible*. To marry or not to marry? To go out nights and listen to a lot of s - - t I'm not interested in, or stay home and hear a lot of s - - t I've heard before. –RICHARD JENI

I'm a great housekeeper. I get divorced. I keep the house. –ZSA ZSA GABOR

Putting a ring on a woman's finger is just like pulling a rip-cord on an inflatable raft. –ETTA MAY

At 38 years, I finally got me the woman that said those six words I wanted all my life to hear. "My dad owns a liquor store." –MARK KLEIN

A couple of nights ago, a wife kicks her husband for no apparent reason. He says, "What the hell's that for?" She says, "That's for being a bad lover." He thinks a minute and he kicks her back. She says, "What the hell's that for?" He says, "That's for knowing the difference." –TOMMY SLEDGE

Ladies, you may think you married the man of your dreams...but 15 years later you're married to a reclining chair that burps. –ROSEANNE

Men believe they already have all the clothes they will ever need, and new ones make them nervous. For example, your average man has 84 ties, but he wears, at most, only three of them. He has learned, through humiliating trial and error, that if he wears any of the other 81 ties, his wife will probably laugh at him. –DAVE BARRY

My husband and I found this great new method of birth control that really, really works.... Every night before we go to bed, we spend an hour with our kids. –ROSEANNE

A friend of mine got married and called. He said, "My wife pays more attention to the baby than me." I said, "It seems to me you got to understand: The baby is a blood relation to your wife. That's her son. You're some guy she met in a bar. She knows it. The kid knows it, and I'm sure they have a good laugh about it when you are at work." –GARRY SHANDLING

You know what the best part of getting married is? Opening the envelopes. That way you get to see how cheap your relatives really are. –JOEY CALLAHAN

When I got married, I got married too young. When the minister said, "You may kiss the bride," my husband yelled, "Ohh GROSS!"

–NANCY NORTON

At a wedding, you never hear a man clearly say, "I do," because we figure we can get out of it later on a technicality. –SINBAD

My wife and I were happy for 20 years. Then we met. –RODNEY DANGERFIELD

I was married at one time. It's not the same as having sex, just an incredible simulation…. We tried to make our marriage work. We got a battery-powered sexual aid. Actually a flashlight. When I was performing, she'd wave it back and forth to create an illusion of motion. –TONY STONE

I love being married. I was single for a long time and I just got so sick of finishing my own sentences. –BRIAN KILEY

Being married or single is a choice we all have to make. It's not a great choice…. It's sort of like when the doctor goes, "Ointment or suppositories?" –RICHARD JENI

I'm on my second marriage. You know you let one guy get away, you're gonna have to build a taller fence and put better food out. –BRETT BUTLER

Marriage was not a guy's idea. You know a woman came up with this and some guy fell for it, hook, line and sinker: "Let me get this straight…I never sleep with anyone else ever again and if things don't work out, you get to keep all my stuff? That's great!" –BOBBY SLAYTON

Men and Women

I really detest movies like *Indecent Proposal* and *Pretty Woman* because they send a message to women that sleeping with a rich man is the ultimate goal—and really, that's such a small part of it. –LAURA KIGHTLINGER

The strangest thing about men, you can organize your tool area but can't keep brown stains out of your underwear. –TIM ALLEN

It's silly for a woman to go to a male gynecologist. It's like going to an auto mechanic who has never even owned a car. –CARRIE SNOW

I love being a woman in the nineties, but I think we are getting our advice from all the wrong people. I just finished my copy of *Vanna Speaks*. –DIANE NICHOLS

I come from a small town whose population never changed. Each time a woman got pregnant, someone left town. –MICHAEL PRITCHARD

I like a woman with a head on her shoulders. I hate necks.

–STEVE MARTIN

Men are superior to women. For one thing, they can urinate from a speeding car. –WILL DURST

You wanna hear my personal opinion on prostitution? If men knew how to do it, they wouldn't have to pay for it. –ROSEANNE

Women are more verbal than men. That's why when you see an elderly couple together, it's always the man who has the hearing aid. –JEFF STILSON

On fake breasts: Women are always saying to us, "You know they ain't real. They are all hard and everything." Do they know we don't care if they are real or not? –ARSENIO HALL

I'm an actress. Just finished a play. *Twelve Angry Men.* It's a one-woman show. –BETSY SALKIND

I like my men the way I like my subway trains: hot, packed, and unloading every three minutes! –JUDY TENUTA

On men: Your lives are less stressful. Do you know this? For one thing, what you are wearing tonight will be in style for the rest of your lives. –CAROL SISKIND

When men get together there's a lot of ego at stake. Ever see two guys meet each other for the first time? Within five minutes, there's a top-it contest of life achievements. The first guy will say something innocuous like, "Yeah, when I was a kid I went to the last game when the Mets won the World Series. Top that." The other guy goes, "Yeah, that's right. I went to Woodstock. Sat on a speaker. Top that." "I'm on a first-name basis with the Unknown Soldier. Top that." "I was the busboy at the Last Supper. Top that." "I remember you. How did you like the tip?" –JOE BOLSTER

Men aren't men until they can get to Sears by themselves. –TIM ALLEN

Whereas a woman longs for one man who can satisfy her every want and need, a man longs for every woman who can satisfy his one need. –JEFF STILSON

If you ladies knew what we were really thinking, you'd never stop slapping us. –LARRY MILLER

I've been traveling so much. I was in Dallas, Texas, doing lesbian comedy at a straight club…. It actually went very well. In five weeks I was never heckled once. 'Course I told 'em if they heckled me, they'd have gay kids. There was one man, though, who had a sort of "moment," and he felt the need to share it with me during my show. He looked at me and said, "Hey, did you get that way because you had some kind of bad sexual experience with a guy?" I'm like, "Yeah— like, if that's all it took, the entire female population would be gay, sir, and I'd be here talking about the weather, all right?" –SUZANNE WESTENHOEFER

I want to have kids. I do. I'm 33 years old, a single woman in the '90s. I think I'm gonna adopt. You know what one of my friends just did? Artificial insemination. That's a scary concept. You know why? I don't want to have coffee with a stranger, never mind have their child. –ROSIE O'DONNELL

Men are lying s - - ts…. I'm an algebra liar. I figure two good lies make a positive. –TIM ALLEN

Women might start a rumor but not a war. –MARGA GOMEZ

I've been on an emotional roller coaster lately. The other day my mood ring exploded. –JANINE DITULLIO

Men are pigs. Aren't we, women? Too bad we own everything—just kidding. –TIM ALLEN

Why can't men get more in touch with their feminine side and become self-destructive? –BETSY SALKIND

Men. You give them an inch, they add it to their own.
–BARBARA SCOTT

I'm glad God gave the Ten Commandments to a man. He didn't really have a choice. A woman would have thought, "I know that's what he said, but I really don't think that's what he meant." –DIANE NICHOLS

Men and women both care about smell, but women go to the trouble to smell good. Men are like, "Does this stink too bad to wear one more time? Maybe I should iron it." –JEFF FOXWORTHY

Girls are much more psychic than guys. They are the first to know if you are going to get laid. –PAUL RODRIGUEZ

Guys are lucky because they get to grow mustaches. I wish I could. It's like having a little pet for your face. –ANITA WISE

On penises: Why do men name them? You hear them saying things like, "Well, Bobby's awake." You never hear women saying things like, "I'm sitting on Margaret." –MARSHA WARFIELD

String bikinis? How do they work? It looks like women are flossing their own ass. –HOWIE MANDEL

Men reach their sexual peak at 18. Women reach their sexual peak at 35. Do you get the feeling God is into practical jokes? We're reaching our sexual peak right around the same time they're discovering they have a favorite chair. –RITA RUDNER

I'm not co-dependent myself, but aren't they great to have around? –BETSY SALKIND

They just caught the first female serial killer in Florida. Eight men. But she didn't kill them. She gained access to their homes, hid the remote controls, so they killed themselves. –ELAYNE BOOSLER

I went shopping last week looking for feminine protection. I looked at all the products and I decided on a .38 revolver. –KAREN RIPLEY

See me. Feel me. Touch me. Pay me. –BARBARA SCOTT

All I have to say about men and bathrooms: They're not real specific. It seems if they hit "something" they're happy. –RITA RUDNER

Don't argue with your mate in the kitchen, because we know where everything is and you don't. –DIANE AMOS

On the men's movement: I thought it was called government. –MARGA GOMEZ

A lot of guys think the larger a woman's breasts are, the less intelligent she is. I think it's the opposite—the larger a woman's breasts are, the less intelligent the men become. –ANITA WISE

My real problem was that I didn't know that girls could do math. See, they didn't discover that till 1980.

–BETSY SALKIND

Women are brilliant. Every woman knows how to do the weirdest things right out of the bucket. Every woman knows how to do that Hindu head wrap with the towel out of the shower. A typhoon couldn't blow that thing off their heads. Ever try to do that? You look like a drunk Iraqi soldier. –TIM ALLEN

For women shopping is a sport, much like deer hunting is to men. They are building a new mall in my town. Last week, women were hanging on the fence yelling at the workmen for taking a lunch break. –JEFF FOXWORTHY

In the United States of America, there are over 25,000 sex phone lines for men. You know how many there are for women? Just three. Apparently for women, if we want someone to talk dirty and nasty to us, we'll just go to work. –FELICIA MICHAELS

For the first time in history, more women have jobs than men. It's a good sign. What's not good is that even though women work all day long, they still come home and clean up about 99 percent of the things you cleaned up around the house. There is still a problem here. Women aren't as proud of their 99 percent as men are of their one. We clean up something—we gonna talk about it all week long. It might be on the news... –JEFF FOXWORTHY

Women think men are led around by their penises. We're not. It points us in a direction, I'll give you that. –GARRY SHANDLING

My mom always said men are like linoleum floors. Lay 'em right and you can walk all over them for 30 years. –BRETT BUTLER

My boyfriend and I the other day saw two guys holding hands. My boyfriend completely freaked. "Eww. That's gross. How disgusting. I'd never do anything like that. How immoral." If I were to show him a picture of two naked women together—"What's missing? Me!" –FELICIA MICHAELS

Some gorgeous dame out there tonight turned to me and said, "Mr. Sledge, what do you prefer? Women with panty-hose or bare legs?" I prefer something in between, lady. –TOMMY SLEDGE

So they had the big Million Man March in Washington. No women were allowed to get involved. I'm glad those guys knew where they were going because if they got lost not one of them was going to ask for directions. –JUDY CROON

Feminism was established to allow unattractive women easier access to the mainstream. –RUSH LIMBAUGH

A man's got to do what a man's got to do...and a woman's got to do what he can't. –RHONDA "PASSION" HANSOME

Cosmopolitan is edited by Helen "Gurley" Brown. Now isn't that a hoot? –DIANE NICHOLS

Men can read maps better than women, 'cause only the male mind could conceive of one inch equaling one hundred miles. –ROSEANNE

A study in the *Washington Post* says that women have better verbal skills than men. I just want to say to the authors of that study, "Duh." –CONAN O'BRIEN

Stephen King writes some scary books. He's coming out with the scariest book he ever wrote, *A Husband with a Mind of Its Own*. Don't get scared, ladies. It's just a fantasy. It will never happen. It will be called *Barbecue Starter*. –ROSEANNE

It's everywhere you look now. You can't even go to the book-store anymore. All the books got the same title—*Good Women, Bad Men*. Watch any afternoon talk show—"Why men don't deserve to live, next on *Donahue*." Pick up a woman's magazine, look at the articles inside—"The Penis: Sex Organ or Birth Defect?" –ROB BECKER

On menstruation: Thank God it's a cycle and not something that increases exponentially. –GARRY SHANDLING

In the last couple of weeks I have seen ads for the Wonder Bra. Is that really a problem in this country? Men not paying enough attention to women's breasts? –JAY LENO

In high school, I wanted to be a feminist, but my boyfriend wouldn't let me.

–DENISE MUNRO

The sexes are so different. Women go out and say, "Before I go to bed with a man, I want to know who he is as a person." Guys are thinking, "Let's get them in bed before they find out who we are." –TONY STONE

My boyfriend, like a lot of men, takes great pride in his car. Honey, his car is detailed, waxed, and vacuumed weekly. My car, on the other hand, looks like a really big purse. –DIANE NICHOLS

I'm at a point where I want a man in my life—but not in my house. Just come in, attach the VCR, and get out.
–JOY BEHAR

The other day on *Donahue* they had men that like to dress up as women. When they do, they can no longer parallel park. –ROSEANNE

I love the women's movement, especially when I'm walking behind it. –RUSH LIMBAUGH

There was a girl knocking on my hotel room door all night last night. I finally had to let her out of my room. –HENNY YOUNGMAN

I'm 44. I haven't been married. The words, "I do." I can't imagine saying that on an altar. I mean even now. I go out. I make love. I'm in bed. Even if I get aroused, my penis is in the shape of a question mark. –RICHARD LEWIS

On Victoria's Secret: I've been there a few times. I'll give you guys a tip: Establish that you're not there looking for something in your size right off. –ROSS SCHAEFFER

My ex-husband is the kind of guy who would watch a fishing show on television and pay attention to it.

—BRETT BUTLER

PMS—it's the first benefit I'll be doing. –GARRY SHANDLING

It's interesting to me when I listen to women talk. I'll give you a caricature of a female conversation: One woman will say something like, "Well, I think the Earth is round." The second one will say, "Well, I think it's flat." And the one in the middle will say, "Well, it's probably round and flat." And they move on. Where in a male conversation, you wouldn't have that. One would say, "I think it's round." One would say, "Flat." And the third one would go, "That guy just said the Earth is flat; you said it was round. And I think he said something about your mother, too." There'd have to be a fight until someone would win. –Rob Becker

I found a mud mask in the bathroom. "Honey, what's this stuff?" "It's mud I put on my face to be beautiful." Hell, I married Swamp Thing. I read the directions on mud mask. "Step #1. Lock face into four-wheel drive." –Killer Beaz

We think we have the greatest weapon in the world against men....It's not sex. Not anymore. Not since they found out that we liked it too. –Diane Nichols

Science magazine came out with a report on the difference between men and women's brains. Apparently women are more controlled by a part of the brain called singletgyrus and men are more controlled by a part of the brain known as the penis. –Jay Leno

There are a lot of nice-looking guys out there tonight. But I know no matter how cute and sexy these guys are, there is always someone somewhere that is sick of them. –Carol Henry

You women ever look at men's bodies like they are meat? Are you ever alone with your girlfriends like, "Look at that baby. USDA choice prime cut. Hmmmm." My body is the part they make hot dogs out of. –Drew Carey

Aren't Your Fifteen Minutes Up Yet?

> *George Burns turned 100 years old today. I don't know the secret to his longevity, but I think I speak for all of us when I say, I hope Pauly Shore doesn't know it either.*
> –NORM MACDONALD

I have come up with a sure-fire concept for a hit television show, which would be called, *A Live Celebrity Gets Eaten by a Shark*. –DAVE BARRY

I'm living here in L.A. to pursue my career. I go on auditions constantly and they really stress me out. I had a nightmare that I was cast in this really horrible sitcom and woke up singing [the imaginary theme song] "She's not wearing any wedding veil, 'cause she's the kind of bride who comes in the mail." –MARGARET CHO

A paternity suit was settled recently when the court ruled that Michael Jackson was not the father of a boy who is now age 10. But I understand Michael is asking for visitation rights. –JAY LENO

Madonna wishes she was me, and she begged me to teach her how to play the squeezebox. But I told her to pull up her pants before the NBA falls out! –JUDY TENUTA

Barbra Streisand recently bought six fur coats at an expensive Fifth Avenue store. Normally that would upset me, but I would rather see Streisand wear fur than see Streisand naked.

–JON STEWART

I want y'all to keep buying En Vogue's records because I don't want En Vogue to turn up later and be the psychic friends.... –ROBIN MONTAGUE

On Charles Manson: I know you're not supposed to advocate the death of a fellow human being, but I think this cat reneged on his membership. –DENNIS MILLER

My father made me watch this Barbara Walters special about this guy, this doctor who cures gay men. He's going around the whole country giving lectures, and he said to Barbara that eventually he is going to make every gay man straight. Barbara looked horrified. "Who's going to do my hair? Who's going to decorate my living room? Save two big queens for me. Just put two on the side. I'll pay for them." –FRANK MAYA

I don't know if I should mention this, but one of the reasons I had so much fun when I was in Los Angeles was because I went to Heidi Fleiss's going-out-of-business sale. –DAVID LETTERMAN

That's a tough name, Brooke Shields. It sounds like a feminine protection product. Ladies, having a heavy-flow day? Try new Brooke Shields…with wings. –ROSIE O'DONNELL

In Hollywood, a marriage is successful if it outlasts milk.

–RITA RUDNER

Remember when Sinéad O'Connor tore up that picture of the Pope on *Saturday Night Live*? Think about it: A little bald guy in a dress is attacked on national television by another little bald guy in a dress. –SIB VENTRESS

When I was growing up, I always wanted to be an actress, but there were no Asian role models. Well, one. "Excuse me. Mr. Eddie's Father." –MARGARET CHO

It's been two days since Kathie Lee sang the National Anthem, and my cats still won't come out from behind the couch. –JON STEWART

I have a theory about Tonya Harding: It's not her fault what happened to her. Anybody named Tonya is not expected to amount to anything. –BRETT BUTLER

Scientists in Africa have just discovered the oldest known human ancestor, born 4.4 million years ago. He is already engaged to Anna Nicole Smith. –NORM MACDONALD

You get the feeling, somewhere along the line, Liberace's parents refused to buy him a class ring? –DENNIS MILLER

On a recent Guns N' Roses album: It should say, "Warning: This album contains reactionary bulls - - t soley put on the album to cause controversy and sell a million f - - - ing more records." –BOBCAT GOLDTHWAIT

Did you see the LaToya Jackson layout? I love it. She said she did it to further her career. Maybe I think differently. I'm thinking, "Singing lessons, baby." –ARSENIO HALL

I saw *The Crying Game* last night and was blown away by the surprise. Who would have thought: Forest Whitaker with an accent? –TIM SIMS

I saw Michael Jackson and Cher the other day and it made me think about people with plastic surgery. Like when they die…does their spirit have the new face or the old one? –STEVE ALTMAN

In a controversial new biography, Liz Taylor reveals she likes her lovemaking loud, rough, and frequent. Coincidentally, that's also how she likes to eat. –NORM MACDONALD

When I taped my show in L.A., I got the chance to go to Aaron Spelling's house. He's a rich guy. He's so rich that his handyman actually is Tim Allen. –BILL MAHER

Her dream: For everyone to come out of the closet in Hollywood so that as an out lesbian I can sleep my way to the top. –LYNDA MONTGOMERY

Hosting the Academy Awards is like being married to Larry King. You know that it's going to be painful, but it will also be over in about three hours. –DAVID LETTERMAN

That show *Kung Fu*—I hated that show because the lead character, David Carradine, wasn't even Chinese. That show should not have been called *Kung Fu*, it should have been called *That Guy's Not Chinese*. –MARGARET CHO

Lorena Bobbitt said her husband didn't satisfy her sexually. Well, honey, if you thought it was bad before… –BRETT BUTLER

Speaking of sawed-off pricks, I was thinking of Rush Limbaugh on the way over here. –BRETT BUTLER

On Rush: People go, "He's not really a reactionary."
Bulls - - t, I was at *Schindler's List* and he started the wave. –BRETT BUTLER

Emo Philips, as you know, is a human Q-tip with a Dorothy Hamill haircut. –JUDY TENUTA

If there is one thing I've learned from watching the legends, it's that comedy is 90 percent perspiration and 10 percent agents' fees. –WAYNE COTTER

Kathie Lee Gifford announced she will no longer continue to co-host the Miss America Pageant. The bad news is she now has that much more time to devote to her singing career. –WILL DURST

My only fear about being a lesbian is that the *National Enquirer* is going to write an article saying I'm really straight. –SUZANNE WESTENHOEFER

A private Los Angeles high school is being renamed for junk bond felon Michael Milken after a $5 million donation. It's a four-year school, but with good behavior you can get out in two. –JAY LENO

I have no fear of Frank Sinatra. I told him, "Drop dead, you low-life bastard. You mean nothing to me." Thank God he wasn't there at the time. –JACKIE MASON

Nancy Reagan has agreed to be the first artificial heart donor.

–ANDREA C. MICHAELS

I love the *Enquirer*. I do. I also like wearing fiberglass underwear sometimes. It's a wonderful magazine. Strange. I put a copy in my cat box and the cat won't s - - t in there….why, that would be redundant! –ROBIN WILLIAMS

Lisa Marie has filed for divorce. According to her attorney she's going to make him pay through the noses. –CONAN O'BRIEN

Yes I am a fashion plate and you are begging to lick me! It's an honor to be trashed by the *Enquirer*, especially since I was on the cover, and I never murdered anyone or slept with Roseanne! –JUDY TENUTA

David Hasselhoff is releasing a new album this week. It's called *And You Thought My Acting Sucked.* –DENNIS MILLER

On Shannen Doherty's wedding: Her friends said it was weird to watch her stand in front of a judge and say, "I do" because usually when she stands in front of a judge she says, "Not guilty." –ARSENIO HALL

I may play the lead in the Lorena Bobbitt story. It will be called *Mrs. Hellfire.* –ROBIN WILLIAMS

On Yoko Ono's singing voice: If it was a fight, they'd stop it. –ROBERT WUHL

> ## Big day in the news. Michael Jackson and George Hamilton have officially crossed lines in the pigmentation flow chart.
>
> –DENNIS MILLER

Steven Tyler? I always get him confused with Carly Simon. They have the same mouth. He must store his cash and jewelry when he's on the road in his mouth, and over the years it spread out. –GARRY SHANDLING

Did you hear about the actress who made it the hard way? She had talent. –SHERYL BERNSTEIN

On a better title for Madonna's book Sex: *If You've Ever Had Doubts I'm a Raving Slut, Voilà!* –DEREK EDWARDS

On Saturday Night Live: I feel like the Native American who accepted the pox-infected blankets from the U.S. Cavalry. –Janeane Garofalo

A lot of people say [Elvis] is alive. Yeah, sure he's alive. Sure. Yeah I've talked to him. He sat next to me on the UFO. It was me, Elvis, and Big Foot. They took a blood sample. They f - - - ed us and let us go. –Drew Carey

According to a study, men whose wives nag them live longer…. In a related story, next week Frank Gifford turns 86. –David Letterman

We don't think Charlton Heston's autobiography is coming out soon. The actor is having trouble coming up with a title so he is offering $1,000 to anyone who can name his book. How about *Gun-Toting Hack with a Bad Rug*? –Dennis Miller

Do I want to be on *Comic Relief?* Does Heidi Fleiss have a sore wrist? –Brett Butler

In a recent interview, *Baywatch*'s Pamela Lee said her therapist has advised her to be more feminine. So she's making arrangements to install a third breast. –Conan O'Brien

Elizabeth Taylor's new fragrance, Black Pearls, is being boycotted by upscale department stores. Presumably it smells too much like Larry Fortensky. –Will Durst

The Menendez brothers' second trial has started. Apparently, their plea is to convince the jury that they were once great football players. –Conan O'Brien

Divine Brown sold her story to the highest-bidding tabloid. What a whore!

—GARRY SHANDLING

I think we're making a step forward, because now rock stars are dying in treatment centers instead of hotel rooms.
—GEORGE CARLIN

Julia Roberts and Lyle Lovett broke up this week. Roberts says that for her the marriage was over when she realized, "I'm Julia Roberts, and he's Lyle Lovett." –NORM MACDONALD

I'm a little confused. I heard—and I'm not clear on this—that Hugh Downs was arrested with a hooker? –DAVID LETTERMAN

To all those people who said my show wouldn't last, I have one thing to say, "Good call!" –JON STEWART

Eighty-three percent of Britons say they forgive Princess Di for her infidelity. Apparently, the other 17 percent haven't gotten a good look at Prince Charles. –CONAN O'BRIEN

A new study shows that one out of every four drivers has fallen asleep at the wheel while on the road. And for half of those, the last thing they remember hearing is, "And now, here's a new one from John Tesh." –DENNIS MILLER

I feel sorry for Elvis Presley—how his family buried him in the backyard. Guess they didn't call him King for nothing.
—DREW CAREY

Richard Lewis. Jon Stewart. Four first names. What are we hiding from? –JON STEWART

Newt Gingrich says that the baseball players and owners should be forced to watch *Field of Dreams*. And if they haven't settled the strike in a month, they should have to watch the rest of Kevin Costner's movies. –BILL MAHER

That Little Itch

It's no longer a question of staying healthy—it's a question of finding a sickness you like.

—JACKIE MASON

Health care in America is too expensive. It's too expensive for the average person. What if you're below average with no health insurance? You might as well call Dr. Kevorkian. –ROBIN MONTAGUE

On hemorrhoids: The examination is humiliating. You go in bent over on a table, your pants around your ankles, and an old man has a finger up your ass. It's a lot like summer camp. –JON STEWART

If you are cross-eyed and have dyslexia, can you see okay? –JOHN MENDOZA

This woman sneezed like 300 times. She said, "There must be something in the air." I said, "Yeah, your germs." –LINDA HERSKOVIC

> I think any guy who films his wife giving birth, she ought to be able to film his hemorrhoid surgery later on. "Look girls, Tony is totally dilated. What a trouper he was!"
>
> –JEFF FOXWORTHY

What's great about aspirin is that no matter how long you suck on it, it never loses its flavor. –GREGG ROGELL

I had a heart attack and I finally got into an ambulance. When I came to, I looked around and saw nothing but white faces and I thought I died and went to white man's heaven. I guess I have to lay around and listen to Lawrence Welk all day. –RICHARD PRYOR

I once heard about a man who never drank and never smoked. He was healthy right up to the time he killed himself. –JOHNNY CARSON

Her opening: I know why you're really clapping. 'Cause finally you are going to hear a Clinton not talk about health care. –KATE CLINTON

The price of Prozac went up 50 percent last year. When they asked Prozac users how they felt about this they said, "Whatever..." –CONAN O' BRIEN

My therapist is so weird. She brings her daughter to my session. I'm like, "What's up with the kid?" "It's career day." That's exciting, huh? –JUDY GOLD

Ever go to an emergency room in the South? They're in no hurry down there. I saw a plaque over the door that read, "Time heals all wounds." –STEVE BLUESTEIN

I recently became a Christian Scientist. It was the only health plan I could afford. –BETSY SALKIND

I'm so wracked with guilt, I don't want to stop therapy because I'm afraid to take the income away from my therapist. He's got kids in college. He relies on me. –TIM HALPERN

On plastic surgery: They can take the fat from your rear and use it to bang out the dents in your face. Now, that's what I call recycling. It gives whole new meaning to dancing cheek to cheek. –ANITA WISE

Did you know that if you laid every cigarette smoker end-to-end around the world more than 67 percent of them would drown? –STEVE ALTMAN

I finally have a dental plan. I chew on the other side. –JANINE DITULLIO

My father's a strange guy. He's allergic to cotton. He has pills he can take, but he can't get them out of the bottle. –BRIAN KILEY

On going to group therapy: I cruised into the banquet room. This guy comes up to me out of nowhere, "I'm experiencing you as being judgmental. I'm experiencing you as not caring for others and being a taker." God, man. Bullseye. How did you know, dude? –PAULY SHORE

I'm looking into a new health insurance plan. I thought—I'm a woman. I should really ask if they cover abortions. Then I remembered, I never have sex and I'm not on the pill. So if I do get pregnant, I'd probably want to have the baby Jesus. –JANINE DITULLIO

I just got out of my 12—step program. I took my 144th step. –TIM HALPERN

After 12 years of therapy, my psychiatrist said something that brought tears to my eyes: "No hablo inglés." –RONNIE SHAKES

The statistics on sanity are that one out of every four Americans is suffering from some form of mental illness. Think of your three best friends. If they are okay, then it's you. –RITA MAE BROWN

I had my cholesterol checked and it's higher than my SATs. I can now get into any college based on my cholesterol check. –GARRY SHANDLING

I was reading how a female spider will eat the male spider after mating. I guess female spiders know that life insurance is easier to collect than child support. –JANINE DITULLIO

> My sister didn't have such a good day. She's asthmatic and in the middle of an attack she got an obscene phone call. The guy on the other end of the line said, "Did I call you or did you call me?"
>
> —JOHN MENDOZA

The dentist told me I grind my teeth at night, so now before I go to sleep I fill my mouth with hot water and coffee beans and set my alarm for 7:30. –JEFF MARDER

I'm terrified of being trapped in a folding bed. I'm a claustropedic. –CAROLYN MAY

I wore a neck brace for about a year. It wasn't an accident or anything. I just got tired of holding my head up. –MARGARET SMITH

Red meat is NOT bad for you. Now blue-green meat. THAT's bad for you! –TOMMY SMOTHERS

I told my doctor I broke my leg in two places. He told me to quit going to those places. –HENNY YOUNGMAN

I was walking down the street wearing glasses when my prescription ran out. –STEVEN WRIGHT

I said to my doctor the other day, "My penis is burning." He said, "That's just because someone is talking about it." –GARRY SHANDLING

If carrots are so good for my eyes, how come I see so many dead rabbits on the highway? –RICHARD JENI

Fear is being stuck in heavy traffic and you just had two cups of coffee and a bran muffin. –JOHN MENDOZA

My body is dropping so fast, my gynecologist wears a hard hat. –JOAN RIVERS

I'm a hypochondriac. At least that's what my gynecologist keeps telling me. –GREGG ROGELL

I quit smoking. I feel better. I smell better. And it's safer to drink out of old beer cans laying around the house. –ROSEANNE

I have a buddy who would call in sick to work and read the back of the Vicks Formula 44D box verbatim: "What's the matter with you, Joe?" "I have symptoms due to runny nose, flu and cough, uh, I may be drowsiness and I, uh, got to keep away from children, yeah." –MARK CURRY

I saw a commercial on TV the other day for Preparation H that said, "Kiss your hemorrhoids goodbye." Not even if I could. –JOHN MENDOZA

Exercise Daily, Eat Wisely, Die Anyway

> *You know, I really don't think I need buns of steel. I'd be happy with buns of cinnamon.*
> —ELLEN DEGENERES

I feel good. I lost 20 pounds on that deal-a-meal plan. Not that Richard Simmons plan. This is where you play cards, lose, and don't have enough cash to eat. –JOHN MCDOWELL

I work so hard to stay in shape. Whenever I read anything it says, "Consult your doctor before doing any exercise." It always says that. Does anybody do that? I kind of think my doctor has people coming in with serious problems. I don't think I should call him and say, "Hi, this is Rita. I'm thinking of bending at the waist." –RITA RUDNER

Human beings are 70 percent water and with some, the rest is collagen.

–MARTIN MULL

You seen these people who are using the Stairmaster. Have we turned into gerbils, ladies and gentlemen? –DENIS LEARY

I have a great diet—you're allowed to eat anything you want, but you must eat it with naked fat people. –ED BLUESTONE

Now you are supposed to keep earthquake preparedness kits. I'm not keeping canned goods in my apartment for an earthquake. If I get trapped beneath a beam for three days, I'm at least going to lose weight. I don't want them finding me miraculously at the end of the week. "Christ, she's huge." "I was miraculously able to get to some beans, thank God." –PAULA POUNDSTONE

My friend is an idiot. He smokes three packs of cigarettes a day. He won't quit either. His big excuse is, "Why should I quit smoking? Anything could kill me. I could be walking down the street one day and I could be hit by a bus." Maybe if you quit smoking you could cross the street a hell of a lot faster. –GREGG ROGELL

> **In my Greenwich Village neighborhood, the men have become so developed that our local supermarket is the only store in the world where the meat section walks up and down the aisles.**
>
> –JAFFE COHEN

It's hard to be famous and struggle with a weight problem. Strangers will tell you to your face what they think. I was in Baskin Robbins a couple of months ago—just looking. Anyway I was there and this lady said to me, "Hey! Are you Rosie O'Donnell?" I said, "Yes I am." She said, "I didn't know you were pregnant." I looked at her and said, "Yes, four and a half months." You shouldn't lie because then she kept asking. "What are you going to name it?" "I don't know, either Ben or Jerry, I'm not sure." –ROSIE O'DONNELL

There's a woman who swam around Manhattan. Someone asked why she did it. She said, "Because no one had ever done it before." Well, she didn't have to do that. If she wanted to do something no one else had ever done before, all she'd have to do is vacuum my apartment. –RITA RUDNER

Did you see this new invention from Chicago? The Sniff Diet. It's an inhaler. Smells like Fritos. When you are hungry you smell it and it tricks your body into thinking you are eating…. Half the people in the study are losing weight. Half the people are eating the inhalers. –TIM BEDORE

Ever notice that they never take any fat hostages? It's always the skinny people. It's never the big fat hellholes that could use the time in captivity. Ever see a guy go, "I was held hostage for seven months but I lost 175 pounds. I look good. I feel good, and I learned self-discipline." No. If Elvis had been held hostage, he'd still be alive today. –DENIS LEARY

I'd hate to be a member of Overeaters Anonymous. It's not like Alcoholics Anonymous where you can hear some wild testimony of drunken debauchery. How exciting can OA testimony be? It's not like you are ever going to hear, "Wow I'm sorry.... I was so full last night I don't remember meeting you." –LAURA KIGHTLINGER

I can't get into that California lifestyle. I was at the beach and every time I would lie down, people would push me back into the water. "Hurry up, he's dying." –LOUIE ANDERSON

I've been doing the Fonda workout: the Peter Fonda workout. That's where I wake up, take a hit of acid, smoke a joint, and go to my sister's house and ask her for money. –KEVIN MEANEY

I joined a health club last year, spent 400 bucks. Haven't lost a pound. Apparently you have to show up. –RICH CEISLER

I feel like a wimp going into a restaurant. What do you want to eat, sir? Broccoli? Broccoli's a side dish. Always has been. Always will. –DENIS LEARY

If I cut myself shaving, sausage gravy comes out. That's why I keep a pile of biscuits next to the sink. –DREW CAREY

Girls, do you retain water? I retain pizzas and Twinkies.
–ETTA MAY

I am indeed shrinking, but that's okay because I can buy my clothes off the rack in the children's department. It's great. There I am at a wedding wearing this gorgeous gown. A five-year-old was wearing the same one. Bitch. –MARLA LUKOFSKY

I tried Slimfast: one delicious shake in the morning and then migraines and diarrhea all day. I hope the Dodgers suffer. Tommy Lasorda selling that stuff. That's why you never see him arguing on the field anymore. –ELAYNE BOOSLER

Nutri/System…What kind of Nazi diet plan is this? This is where they tell you you have to eat the food they make. They tell you what time of day you have to eat it and you have to eat all of it. This isn't a diet. This is living with your parents. –DESTINY

Fat people don't think like thin people. We have our own way of thinking different. Did you ever go up to a fat person on the street and ask them where something is? They tell you—like this is where the difference really shows. "Well, go down here to Arby's. Go right past Wendy's, McDonald's, Burger King, Taco Bell, Kentucky Fried Chicken. It's the chocolate brown building." –ROSEANNE

I used to wear a "3." Of course, I was a fetus at the time.
–ETTA MAY

Either I'm losing weight or I'm getting so fat that I'm scaring the s - - t out of my clothes. –BARRY DIAMOND

I'm not into working out. My philosophy: No pain, no pain.
–CAROL LEIFER

One wonders what we did with our time before we decided to spend every spare moment at the gym. I, too, have succumbed to the pressure. Yesterday, I spent a full hour grunting and groaning at the Nautilus machine. And then—after I finally got the seat adjusted—I actually worked out for five minutes. –JAFFE COHEN

You want my recipe for trail mix? Plain M&Ms. Kraft Caramels. Peanut M&Ms. It gets me over the mountain. –ROSEANNE

Celery has negative calories. It takes more energy to chew it than the food contains. I was thinking about this: If you eat 30 pounds of celery for seven days, you could disappear. The seventh day you are kind of chomping away, getting kind of transparent, getting a green hue, kind of going Poof! –TIM BEDORE

I went on a diet. Had to go on two diets at the same time 'cause one diet wasn't giving me enough food. –BARRY MARTER

It's not nice to talk about fat people, but f--k it. They can't catch you.

–MARSHA WARFIELD

Only Irish coffee provides in a single glass all four essential food groups: alcohol, caffeine, sugar, and fat. –ALEX LEVINE

I live alone. I'm not married. I hope to be someday so I can stop exercising. –JEFF STILSON

On Slimfast: Their slogan is, "Give us a week, we'll take off the weight." Liars. Why don't they tell the truth? "Give us a week. We'll give you the runs. When you are strong enough, you'll eat solids again." –DESTINY

The cat was not safe when I was on Slimfast. I swear to God. I was chasing the cat. I had soy sauce in one hand, chopsticks in the other. I was like, "Come here, you little bastard. Mommy's hungry…Oh, I'm sorry, Fluffy. I snapped." –LINDA SMITH

> When it comes to my health, I think of my body as a temple…or at least a moderately well managed Presbyterian Youth Center.
>
> –EMO PHILIPS

It's always the yogurt, sprout-eatin' motherf- - -ers get run over by a bus driven by a guy who smokes three-and-a-half packs a day. –DENIS LEARY

The reason Oprah lost all that weight is because she has millions of dollars. If I had millions of dollars, I'd pay someone a million dollars a day to smack the Doritos out of my hand. –BECKY DONOHUE

I've taken up meditation. I like to have espresso first to make it more challenging. –BETSY SALKIND

On marathons: What would make 17,000 people want to run 26 miles? All I could figure out was maybe there was a Hare Krishna in back of them going, "Excuse me. Could I talk to you for just a second?" –RITA RUDNER

Friends Don't Let Friends Beer Goggle

When I read about the evils of drinking, I gave up reading.
–HENNY YOUNGMAN

Schnapps—the crack of alcohol. –DENIS LEARY

They say they are going to call you at about seven o'clock. It's seven and they haven't called. So you say, okay, I'll fix myself a drink. So you have a drink, then you have another, then you have another, and you have another. Now you're drunk. It's five after seven and they haven't called. –ELLEN DEGENERES

Some people say that a drunk woman is worse than a drunk man. I don't believe in that. I don't care who you are. If you throw up on my shoes, I'm gonna punch your f - - - ing lights out. –MARSHA WARFIELD

I like the designated driver program. Anything is safer than the way we used to do it, "Hey dude, get up, give us a ride home, man…."–JEFF FOXWORTHY

I had to stop drinking alcohol because I used to wake up nude on the hood of my car with my keys up my ass. –ROBIN WILLIAMS

They are trying to put warning labels on liquor. "Caution: Alcohol can be dangerous to pregnant women." Did you read that? That's ironic. If weren't for alcohol, most women wouldn't even be that way. –RITA RUDNER

You know how you tell if the teacher is hung over? Movie Day. –JAY MOHR

I took my uncle to his first Alcoholics Anonymous meeting. I went but we ended up at a Triple A meeting by mistake. We didn't know it. Everyone is sitting there filling out forms and reading maps. We're looking there going, "How is this going to help?" My uncle, the trouper, stood up and said, "My name is Frank and I'm an alcoholic." They all looked up and said, "You shouldn't be driving" and went right back to the maps. –BILLIAM CORONEL

Hey bartender, a thousand pints of light! –SECOND CITY PLAYERS

I hate to start on a serious note, but I do want to take some time to thank some people. This has been a very difficult week for me since my show was canceled. There is someone I'd like to thank. My two good friends: Jack Daniels and Perc O. Dan.

–JON STEWART

You know when you are drunk and you are weirdly optimistic? –JANEANE GAROFALO

I was in a bar the other night hopping from barstool to barstool, trying to get lucky—there wasn't any gum under any of them. –EMO PHILIPS

On the bus: The guy in front of me went into convulsions, started swallowing his tongue, shaking, sweating and puking. His friend was with him and he was like, "Oh man, he was drinking for 55 days straight. We got to get him off the bus now." We stop, get him off the bus, and I'm thinking, "Oh, great. Now who is going to drive?" –KATHLEEN MADIGAN

My inner child is grounded until he learns to handle his liquor. It apparently had a couple of tequilas last night and told a cop to go f - - k himself. –TIM CONLON

On the Coors Lite talking can: I find that if you have enough beer, each can starts to talk to you anyway. –ROB ROSS

> I like to get drunk too. All the way to throwing-up time. Then I don't like that s- -t no more. That's when I start saying real stupid things like, "I shouldn't have had that last one." Like that's the one that did it. The first 17 I had don't count? That last one f- - ked me up.
>
> –MARSHA WARFIELD

Have you ever gotten so drunk you use a barstool as a walker to get home? –WINSTON SPEAR

A lot of things go on when you're a kid that you don't figure out until you're an adult. Like, I think my kindergarten teacher had a drinking problem, because nap time was every day from nine o'clock to two-thirty. –JANINE DITULLIO

The problem with the designated driver program is it's not a desirable job. But if you ever get sucked into doing it, have fun with it. At the end of the night, drop them off at the wrong house. –JEFF FOXWORTHY

I used to be a bartender at the Betty Ford Clinic. –STEVEN WRIGHT

I once got drunk and threw up so much that it went back to things I ate when I was in the 9th grade...Red Hots, Snickers, and at least one cheat sheet. –DARRELL HAMMOND

I woke up this morning to the smell of coffee, bacon on the griddle, pancakes being made. I looked around. G - - dammit! I passed out in Denny's again! –MARK KLEIN

When I was in college, we used to watch *The Love Boat*. We played a drinking game where everyone picks a character at the beginning of the show and whenever that person appeared in the show you would take a drink. You could always tell who the alcoholics in your group were because they would say, "I want to be the boat." –MARGARET CHO

Modern Maturity

You're not a kid anymore when you can live without sex, but not without your glasses.
—JEFF FOXWORTHY

If you are planning on buying tickets to the next Rolling Stones tour, I've got some information you can use. You can charge the tickets to your MasterCard, Visa card, and Sears card. They will also accept third-party-endorsed Social Security checks. –DAVID LETTERMAN

Women are having children much later in life. I read an article in *New York* magazine: Women 49 years old having their first child. Forty-nine. I couldn't think of a better way to spend my golden years. What's the advantage of having kids at 49? You can both be in diapers at the same time? –SUE KOLINSKY

You're not a kid anymore when you are obsessed with the thermostat. –JEFF FOXWORTHY

Since I passed 30, I have acquired a taste for things I never liked before—like younger men. I'm only 33, so younger than me is paper-boy age. "No son, I want my paper delivered inside the house from now on. Don't argue with me...I have cookies...Find them." –MARSHA WARFIELD

The only reason I would take up jogging is so I could hear heavy breathing again.

–ERMA BOMBECK

Al Roker is taking over Willard Scott's job on the *Today* show. Don't feel bad for Willard, though. He just made $2 million selling his list of 100-year-olds to Dr. Kevorkian. –CONAN O'BRIEN

Middle age is when your age starts to show around your middle. –BOB HOPE

I have to tell you, the older I get, the more eating replaces sex. Last weekend I installed a mirror over the dining room table. –RODNEY DANGERFIELD

You get a little perspective when you pass 30. I'm beginning to appreciate the value of naps. Naps are wonderful. It's like what was I fighting all these years? –MARSHA WARFIELD

At my age, sex is sensational. Especially, the one in the winter. –MILTON BERLE

You know you are getting old when the candles cost more than the cake. –BOB HOPE

My folks just moved to Florida this year, but they didn't want to move to Florida. But they're in their sixties and that's the law. –JERRY SEINFELD

Some people say older men have long endurance and can make love longer. Let's think about this. Who wants to f - - k an old man for a long time? –MARSHA WARFIELD

Death is just a distant rumor to the young. –ANDY ROONEY

You're not a kid anymore when nobody wants to see your cleavage. –JEFF FOXWORTHY

I'm starting to worry more about getting Alzheimer's than AIDS…but for the life of me I can't remember why. –ANITA MILNER

I don't talk about my hair anymore because I've matured and realized, looks aren't important. It's about what kind of hair you have inside. –GARRY SHANDLING

I'm so old I can remember when AT&T was just called "A."
–PHYLLIS DILLER

No one in my family ages well. I think somebody peed in our gene pool. –RICK SCOTTI

You know you are getting old when people tell you how good you look. –ALAN KING

On his father: He's just incredible. He does 45 minutes on the treadmill a day. He's on his stomach. It's like a loofah. –BOB SAGET

The older I get the more sleazy everything seems. –MARK FARRELL

> One of the powers of adulthood is the ability to be totally bored and remain standing. That's why they could set up the DMV that way.
>
> –JERRY SEINFELD

How young can you die of old age? –STEVEN WRIGHT

I'm getting old. When I squeeze into a tight parking space, I'm sexually satisfied for the day. –RODNEY DANGERFIELD

Modern Times

USA Today
*has come out with a new survey—
apparently three out of every four people
make up 75 percent of the population.*
–DAVID LETTERMAN

Kids Today...

I worry about kids today. Because of the sexual revolution, they're going to grow up and never know what "dirty" means. –LILY TOMLIN

I was listening to some rap music this afternoon. Not that I had a choice—it was coming out of a Jeep four miles away. –NICK DEPAULO

This is a reminder that if you want to get your back-to-school gift in time for your favorite student, you now have to allow for the five-day waiting period. –GREG KINNEAR

I think about a lot of sick things. Do you know how f - - - ed up science class will be for test tube babies? Think about it. That's where you find out your father jacked off in a jar. Your mother was a petri dish. You wind up with a kid with a real strong urge to masturbate in front of girls with bifocals. –MARSHA WARFIELD

Our bombs are smarter than the average high school student. At least they can find Kuwait. –A. WHITNEY BROWN

Single people throw the best parties. They don't have to worry about their furniture getting messed up. Their friends can destroy everything they own. They're out 15 bucks. –JEFF FOXWORTHY

We used to terrorize our babysitters when I was little, except for my grandfather because he used to read to us...from his will. –JANINE DITULLIO

I had to quit university because my Dungeons and Dragons character died. –AL RAE

My brother's name is Greg, but when he got out of college he changed his name to Mkazi, which means "He who runs from student loan people." –TONY EDWARDS

Hitler had only one testicle. It's true. You use facts like that to make class more interesting. But that's the only thing kids remember from that class. So you have a history test and the question is, "The Causes of World War II" and the kid writes, "Hitler had only one nut." –STEVE BRINDER

I found something a lot more scary than cocaine. Nintendo—kiddy cocaine. –ROBIN WILLIAMS

People want to take sex education out of the schools. They believe sex education causes promiscuity—if you have the knowledge, use it. Hey, I took algebra. I never do math.

—ELAYNE BOOSLER

They say teaching sex education in the public schools will promote promiscuity. With our educational system? If we promote promiscuity the same way we promote math or science, they've got nothing to worry about. –BEVERLY MICKINS

When I was in high school we would give each other hickeys and then make up fictitious boyfriends that gave them to us. It never occurred to us that we were real. –BETSY SALKIND

On marijuana: Can you imagine what the sticker would be like if they legalized it? "Warning: Marijuana is a major cause of Woodstock II." –DAN KELLY

I hated math. Math teachers would ask me questions. "Mr. Kinney, can you tell us the common denominator here?" Yeah, we all think this sucks. –DAVID KINNEY

We spend so much money on the military, yet we're slashing education budgets throughout the country. No wonder we've got smart bombs and stupid f - - king children. –JON STEWART

Nintendo is coming out with what they say is the most violent video game ever made. It's called, *The Super Menendez Brothers*. –JAY LENO

Green Piece(s)

I just got junk mail from this organization that wants me to save the forest. I sent them back a letter saying stop sending me the junk mail and save the forest yourself. –LINDA HERSKOVIC

Environmentalists want forests to stay so that they can grow pot without detection. –RUSH LIMBAUGH

I'm doing what I can to help the environment. I started a compost pile. It's in the back seat of my car. –JANINE DITULLIO

On recycled paper: I feel that the wrapper on my McDonald's hamburger might once have been toilet paper. –BECKY DONOHUE

Earth Day was held recently. In honor of that event, I decided that I am going to use only recycled jokes. –DAVID LETTERMAN

Remember when you were considered an environmentalist when you didn't throw junk out of the car window? I sure do miss that happier, simpler time. –PAULA POUNDSTONE

Money—and the Lack Thereof

Don't spend $2 to dry clean a shirt. Donate it to the Salvation Army instead. They'll clean it and put it on a hanger. Next morning buy it back for 75 cents. –BILLIAM CORONEL

I bought the Encyclopedia Britannica on 30-day trial offer. Thank God. It took me that long to Xerox it. –LINDA HERSKOVIC

I have enough money to last me for the rest of my life unless I buy something. –JACKIE MASON

A bank is a place that will lend you money if you can prove that you don't need it. –BOB HOPE

I had a hard time at the bank today, I tried to take out a loan and they pulled a real attitude with me. Apparently, they won't accept the voices in my head as references. –STEVE ALTMAN

Yeah, you so poor you can't even pay attention. –DAMON WAYANS

You know you're poor when you start to envy people with bus passes. –BONNIE MCFARLANE

A bank teller didn't recognize me. He said, "I need to see two pieces of ID, Mr. Sledge." So I tore my driver's license in half. –TOMMY SLEDGE

Last month I had to borrow $500 from a very good friend of mine. She lends me the money. Three days later she calls me freaking out about her job and at one point she says she wants to kill herself. All I can think is, "Why are you telling me? I owe you $500." What am I supposed to say, "Don't do it"? –JESSICA BURR

We were poor. You know when you take off your socks and you got that little bit of lint caught in your toenails? My mommy saved that and made me a sweater for Christmas. My daddy had a belly-button leisure suit. –RONNIE BULLARD

Money is better than poverty if only for financial reasons. –WOODY ALLEN

Shopping

There is a way to find out if a salesman at the Gap is gay. Very simple. Just ask him to name the colors of the things in the store. –SCOTT CAPURRO

I watch that Home Shopping Club. They've got the tools from hell on that show. The salesmen are good. "Folks, folks, folks—eliminate the worry of sharpening scissors at home." Forget that check to Greenpeace, hon. There's a major problem right here! –TIM ALLEN

I had to go shopping at the tall girls shoe shop. Two floors of tall girls shoes. There was a basketball court in the basement in case anyone wanted to shoot hoops. –JUDY GOLD

I don't buy products that they test on animals because I like to test on them myself. –LINDA HERSKOVIC

Veni, vidi, Visa. (We came, we saw, we went shopping.) –JAN BARRETT

When I was a kid a "crack salesman" just meant a guy was really good at what he did. –BOBBY SLAYTON

I went to a bookstore the other day. I asked the woman behind the counter where the self-help section was. She said, "If I told you that would defeat the whole purpose." –BRIAN KILEY

Modern Conveniences

We live in an age when pizza gets to your home before the police. –JEFF MARDER

It says a lot about your life what you have on your speed dial. I have two things on my speed dial and I get them confused: the take-out chicken place and the suicide hotline. You don't know what it's like to be bawling your eyes out for 20 minutes and some lady breaks in, "You want the nine-piece bucket or the 12-piece bucket?" I don't know how many times I've called the suicide hotline to see what's holding my chicken up. –JOAN KEITER

The detergent Tide is improved. They are still working on Tide. –JERRY SEINFELD

Lotta self-help tapes out there. Got one called *How to Handle Disappointment*. I got it home and the box was empty. –JONATHAN DROLL

The Gerber Company is in big trouble. They had to recall 10 million pacifiers. It seemed a *Consumer Reports* study came out saying they sucked. –CONAN O'BRIEN

I called the Psychic Friends hotline, we spoke for six hours, and she did not realize that I wasn't going to pay my bill. –MICHAEL ARONIN

Why do they sell lemon juice made with artificial ingredients and lemon floor polish made with real lemon juice? Now I drink tea with a twist of Mop 'n Glow. –BOBBY KELTON

Now they show you how detergents take out bloodstains, a pretty violent image there. I think if you've got a T-shirt with bloodstains all over it, maybe laundry isn't your biggest problem. Maybe you should get rid of the body before you do the wash. –JERRY SEINFELD

Spent the afternoon listening to self-improvement tapes. Now I'm feeling a little inadequate. I don't have the CDs. –DENNIS MILLER

Only in America would a guy invent crack. Only in America would there be a guy that cocaine wasn't good enough for, y'know? –DENIS LEARY

Computers make it easy to do a lot of things, but most of the things they make it easier to do, don't need to be done. –ANDY ROONEY

The day I worry about cleaning my house is the day Sears comes out with a riding vacuum cleaner. –ROSEANNE

On psychic phone sex: "What are you wearing? No, wait, don't tell me." –TIM SEEVES

How dangerous could anything named "Foamy" be? Hell, you could name your poodle Foamy. But on this shave cream it now says: "Warning: Keep away from open flame." You know what that means. Sometime in the past, some nut has said to his wife, "Honey, I think I'll sit in the fireplace to shave." –JAMES GREGORY

Sears Toughskins—reversible, polyester, ugly pants. Your knees will wear out before the pants do. –TIM ALLEN

"Buffet" is a French term. It means get up and get it yourself. –GREG RAY

See, if the plane crashes in the ocean, the seats will float. La-dee-da. There's no water from here to Atlanta. If you want me to tie my seatbelt, show me a seat that's going to bounce off one of those mountains down there. –JAMES GREGORY

I put instant coffee in my microwave oven and almost went back in time. –STEVEN WRIGHT

Promotable, Demotable You

AT&T this week announced the first 40,000 layoffs. A spokesman for AT&T said, "You know anyone who needs a good spokesman?" –NORM MACDONALD

I used to work at a woman's correctional home. All the inmates worked, it wasn't just me. –LINDA HERSKOVIC

I tried to make money as a kid. I had a lemonade stand for about six weeks. I made no money. I had to burn it down and collect insurance. –BRIAN KILEY

The Idiot Box

They said Saddam Hussein used to sit around and watch CNN. On top of every horrible thing he's done, he has an illegal cable hook-up. –GARRY SHANDLING

It's hard to decide if TV makes morons out of everyone or if it mirrors Americans who are morons to begin with. –MARTIN MULL

If it weren't for Philo T. Farnsworth, inventor of television, we'd still be eating frozen radio dinners. –JOHNNY CARSON

Don't you wish there were a knob on the TV to turn up the intelligence? There's one marked brightness, but it doesn't work. –GALLAGHER

MTV is the lava lamp of the 1980s. –DOUG FERRARI

I don't know what's wrong with my television set. I had it on the same station. I was getting C-Span and the Home Shopping Network. I actually bought a Congressman. –BRUCE BAUM

Who says we didn't have controversial subjects on TV back in my time? Remember *Bonanza*? It was about three guys in high heels living together. –MILTON BERLE

I watched *thirtysomething* totally by mistake. I thought it was a really long Nissan ad. –BOBCAT GOLDTHWAIT

Some guy broke into our house last week. He didn't even take the TV. He just took the remote control. Now he drives by and changes channels on us. –BRIAN KILEY

I'm really excited. I'm gonna be in a TV commercial. I was in an accident in a Volvo and I sent them a letter for saving my life... Let me read it for you: "Dear Volvo, You saved our life. I was jerking my boyfriend Larry off on the way to a Dead concert. He climaxed and we hit a guard rail and went down over a steep embankment. I was so dusted I thought I was dead. My punishment in hell was to eat out Roseanne. Lucky for me it was just the airbag. Thanks Volvo, you saved our life." Joan Keiter, NYC. –JOAN KEITER

And...

Unlike the Reagans, the homeless have not gone away.
–WHOOPI GOLDBERG

I saw a bag lady the other day. She was wearing an orange taffeta ball gown. It was unzipped down the back and hanging kind of low in the front. Apparently, a lot of homeless people are prom dates who never made it home. –JANINE DiTULLIO

I was walking with Mayor Tom Bradley—it could happen—the Mayor said, "Judy, you don't think we have too many homeless people?" I said, "Oh, no. It's perfectly normal for the sidewalk to be so soft." –JUDY TENUTA

On the Gulf War: How long did the war last? 100 hours? The ground war lasted 100 hours. People were afraid it was going to be another Vietnam. It wasn't even a Woodstock. –JON STEWART

The Contras are breaking up. Apparently one of them is dating Yoko Ono. –DENNIS MILLER

On gays in the military: What's the army afraid is going to happen if gay people are in it? "Private, shoot this man." "I can't. He's adorable. Blue eyes and that uniform. It's too much." I think the army is afraid of 10,000 guys with M-16's going, "Who'd you call faggot?" –JON STEWART

What's it going to be like in 30, 40, 50 years? It'll be like, "Sir, you can take your driving test in Spanish, English, or Dude." "S - - t, I'll take it in Dude, dude." –PAULY SHORE

Universal Studios has the Earthquake ride now, which is a very important thing to have. The Ten Plagues ride is coming in a few weeks. –BOB SAGET

I think 'ludes explain why we were wearing the giant flare bell-bottom pants and the platform shoes. What do you think? I think it's the only possible explanation. There we were, in the middle of a sexual revolution, wearing clothing that guaranteed we wouldn't get laid. –DENIS LEARY

You never know what guttersnipe is waiting for you out in the alley. I'm telling all my girlfriends to get into defensive dressing. Believe me, no one comes near you when you are wearing an electric fence. Why not try wearing a live German shepherd around your neck? It's safe and chic at the same time. –SANDRA BERNHARD

I'm a little bit femme and little bit butch. I wear makeup...but I keep it in a tackle box.

–LYNDA MONTGOMERY

I just want you to know that there is such a thing as a Gay Mafia.... Be careful or they will break the legs on your coffee table. –BOB SMITH

I do clean up a little. If company is coming, I'll wipe the lipstick off the milk container. Comb the soap. –ELAYNE BOOSLER

The Superhighway? That sounds like a place that's long and boring and kills 50,000 people a year. –DICK CAVETT

It's amazing that the amount of news that happens in the world everyday just exactly fits the newspaper. –JERRY SEINFELD

My boyfriend works for a driving school. One of the great perks is you get to take the car out on the weekend. I'm telling you that's one great party car. You can be doing lines of coke, smoking joints, be drunk out of your head, swerving all over the road. No one ever says anything. Even the cops say, "Get a load of the student driver." –JOAN KEITER

You know when you step on a mat in the supermarket and the door opens? For years, I thought it was a coincidence. –RICHARD JENI

One time I was working a nightclub and had to park far away. I'm walking to the club past a garage door with one of those signs. "Don't Even Think About Parking Here." Like people aren't tense enough about the parking thing. Someone has to put up a smartass sign. "Don't Even Think About Parking Here." I tell you what. I stood there and thought about it. I did. I threw some pebbles up there to get their attention. "Look. I'm thinking about it. Go ahead, call the cops and see if I care. I'll tell them I'm thinking about something else." –PAULA POUNDSTONE

I did so much crack one day I broke into my own house. I was halfway out the door with the TV before I realized it was my place. Before I broke in, I used to stand outside and case the joint going, "Damn, this brother ain't never coming home." –MICHAEL COLYAR

Do you think that Beethoven ever did a bad song? He was such a genius. Did Beethoven ever sit down at the piano and go, "Everybody was Kung Fu fighting?"

–ARSENIO HALL

If you surveyed a hundred typical middle-aged Americans, I bet you'd find that only two of them could tell you their blood types, but every last one of them would know the theme song from the *Beverly Hillbillies*. –DAVE BARRY

On citizen's arrest: That's your right as a citizen. You can arrest people. I'd like to thank the government for that one. How in the hell am I supposed to exercise that right? I guess they give it to me in case I get particularly pissed off at some criminal I can just walk up to the guy, "Okay, drop the gun. I can't take it no more. Let's go. Get in the car. Don't worry about who I am. I live here." Who the hell are you supposed to call for backup? "Mom and Dad. Come here. Let's go." –MARIO JOYNER

I have six locks on my door all in a row. When I go out, I only lock every other one. I figure no matter how long some-body stands there picking the locks, they are always locking three. –ELAYNE BOOSLER

On gays in the military: If we wanted to be part of an institution that is hostile to gays and women, we'd just stay home with our families. –GEORGIA RAGSDALE

I came to a 7-Eleven. I stopped. I stared. It didn't add up.

—TOMMY SLEDGE

The bus scares me. Way too many gross people on the bus. Sixty-five people on the bus and I was the last one on. I felt like calling *Unsolved Mysteries*. "Yeah, I found everybody." –KATHLEEN MADIGAN

On women's marches: I have friends who say, "Come to the women's march, take off your shirt, liberate yourself." I can't do that. I'm afraid of people's response. I'm afraid they'll go, "Look at that little boy. What's that little boy doing at the women's march? That's so sad. He must be homeless. Let's march for him." –BECKY DONOHUE

Not the Bradys

I will never forget the day my grandmother died... mostly because I won the pool.
–BRENT CUSHMAN

Adults ask children what they want to be when they grow up 'cause they are looking for ideas. –PAULA POUNDSTONE

Boy, parents—there's a tough job. Damn easy job to get, though. I think most people love the interview. You don't have to dress for it. –STEVE BRUNER

On baby intercoms: She's in the crib with one part of the intercom and I'm in the other room. "Breaker one-nine. Daddy, I got spitup on my shirt and I'm packing a load. Please come in and help me." –BOB SAGET

My parents put a live teddy bear in my crib. –WOODY ALLEN

I took my parents back to the airport today...they leave tomorrow.

–MARGARET SMITH

My son is into that nose-picking thing. The least he can do is act like an adult—buy a car and sit in traffic. –ROSEANNE

My mother just wrote her autobiography. Pick it up. It's in the stores right now. It's entitled, *I Came. I Saw. I Criticized.* –JUDY GOLD

Once you survive growing up, the next step is to have your own kid.... It's a major point. I think you are at a certain level when everyone you know pretty much has caught on to you. You need to create a new person, someone who does-n't know anything about you....You have a kid, the relation-ship is off to a great start. You give the kid food and toys, and immediately they are very impressed with you.
–JERRY SEINFELD

If your parents never had children, chances are you won't either. –DICK CAVETT

Moms will clean up everything. Scientists have proven that a mom's spit is the exact chemical composition of Formula 409. Mom's spit on a Kleenex. You get rust off a bumper with that thing. –JEFF FOXWORTHY

My father's a proctologist. My mother is an abstract artist. That's how I view the world. –SANDRA BERNHARD

I want to adopt a child. Not a baby, one with a job. –LINDA HERSKOVIC

When I first came out to my family—you probably all had this experience—they shunned me. You know, when I think back to that time, I kind of liked it. –KATE CLINTON

I'm a Jewish girl who was raised in a vegetarian family. My dream is to open a restaurant called "Soy Vey." –MARGO BLACK

Even when freshly washed and relieved of all obvious confections, children tend to be sticky. –FRAN LEBOWITZ

When I lived here I drove a '65 Mustang—my best friend, "Dave." It was a great car, but it broke down all the time. I figured someday it was going to break down and I'd break down. They'd find me on the side of the road yelling at it like I was its parent. "Do you have any idea of how much money I've put into you this month alone? I give and give and give. Could you maybe take me two or three miles. Oh no. Look at all the other cars. They are moving. You had to have new brake shoes. I buy them for you. You don't wear them…"
–PAULA POUNDSTONE

Me and my dad used to play tag—he'd drive! –RODNEY DANGERFIELD

On her imagined Academy Award acceptance speech: I'd like to thank my mother and my father for providing me with the need to seek the love of strangers. –BETSY SALKIND

I just got engaged. I'm about to marry a gentile. That makes my parents...dead. –JESSICA BURR

I just got back from visiting my family....I show up at the door and this is how my mother greeted me. "Honey, you are not coming in the house in that baggy jacket. Why don't you give it to some fat person?" I said, "Ya know, if you want the jacket..." –JANINE DITULLIO

When the family first comes to visit, quite frankly what I did was "de-dyke" the apartment. You know it—we call it straightening up. –KATE CLINTON

We had natural childbirth. We had her [our baby] on a bed of lettuce at the Sizzler. –BOB SAGET

My husband and I are either going to buy a dog or have a child. We can't decide whether to ruin our carpet or ruin our lives. –RITA RUDNER

I've noticed that the one thing about parents is that no matter what stage your child is in, the parents who have older children always tell you the next stage is worse. –DAVE BARRY

On the Menendez brothers: My father saw this story; he quit playing the lottery. "F - - k, I got 12 kids. Any one of them could snap!" –PAUL RODRIGUEZ

It goes without saying that you should never have more children than you have car windows. –ERMA BOMBECK

I want to have children and I know my time is running out. I want to have them while my parents are still young enough to care for them. –RITA RUDNER

> ## My brother's a taxidermist. You know, he mounts animals. Well, that's how he met my sister-in-law.
>
> –JOHNNY RIZZO

Sears used to be a punishment. My mom would get mad at us. "You've lit your little sister on fire for the last time. I'm taking you boys to Sears and buying you some dress slacks." NOOOO! I'd rather have my balls pounded flat with a wooden hammer. I swear to God. –TIM ALLEN

Human beings are the only creatures that allow their children to come back home. –BILL COSBY

If your child thinks he wants "Murderous Bob, the Doll with the Face You Can Rip Right Off," you'd better get it. You may be worried that it might help to encourage your child's antisocial tendencies, but believe me, you have not seen antisocial tendencies until you've seen a child who is convinced that he or she did not get the right gift. –DAVE BARRY

On her parents: They did a really scary thing recently. They bought a Winnebago. This means they can pull up in front of my house anytime now and just live there....They're not getting any water and they are not plugging anything in. –PAULA POUNDSTONE

Actually I gained my sense of humor from my mother 'cause when I was growing up, she refused to bake. She said, "Well, you just eat it." –BETSY SALKIND

My family's house was built like the Suffer Dome. It's the House That Guilt Built. When I was growing up, I kept my front door open so that I could get cross-humiliation from my brother and sister. –RICHARD LEWIS

My mother I can talk to when I have a problem. My father I call with a problem and he turns into Ed McMahon. "Dad, I'm really upset. I don't know what to do," and he's like, "Here's Mommy!" –JUDY GOLD

I descended from a very long line my mother once foolishly listened to. –PHYLLIS DILLER

I don't think I'll ever have a mother's intuition. My sister left me alone in a restaurant with my 10-month-old nephew. I said, "What do I do if he cries?" She said, "Give him some vegetables." It turns out jalapeño is not his favorite. –JANINE DITULLIO

My mother wants grandchildren, so I said, "Mom, go for it!" –SUE MURPHY

My mother from time to time puts on her wedding dress. Not because she's sentimental. She just gets really far behind in her laundry. –BRIAN KILEY

My mom is totally into getting me married…. She called to find out what's new and I'll say, "I saw Lenny Kravitz." She'll say, "Kravitz, have I met him?" –LYNN HARRIS

This Thanksgiving is gonna be a special one. My mom says I don't have to sit at the card table. –JIM SAMUELS

I'm going home next week. It's kind of a family emergency. My family is coming here. –RITA RUDNER

Fatherhood is pretending that the present you love most is soap-on-a-rope.

–BILL COSBY

I remember my first day of school. My parents dropped me off at the wrong nursery. I didn't know anybody—I was surrounded by trees. –JANINE DITULLIO

My mom said she learned how to swim. Someone took her out in the lake and threw her off the boat. That's how she learned to swim. I said, "Mom, they weren't trying to teach you how to swim." –PAULA POUNDSTONE

On talking with her parents about her personal life: I told them I was gay. I'm going out with this guy that they hate. Now when they meet him, they'll love him. –MARGARET SMITH

I lost my parents at the beach when I was a kid. I asked a lifeguard to help me find them. He said, "I don't know, kid, there are so many places they could hide." –RODNEY DANGERFIELD

My mother hated me. My mother used to say to me, "Take candy from strangers. Ask the guy over there in the raincoat if he owns a van." –JOAN RIVERS

My mother used to tell me things. She had natural childbirth. I recently found out it was her version of natural childbirth. She took off her makeup. –RITA RUDNER

You get a lot of tension. You get a lot of headaches. I do what it says on the aspirin bottle: Take two and keep away from children. –ROSEANNE

When you look at Prince Charles, don't you think that someone in the Royal Family knew someone in the Royal Family? –ROBIN WILLIAMS

I have one brother I borrowed so much money from he's like a human credit card. I go into a store with a picture of him and say, "You take Fred?" –SUE KOLINSKY

I did a special show recently and all four of my parents came and sat together. Cool. It's the first time they'd all been together in the same room since my graduation. Different stepmother, though. Julie couldn't make it that night. She was across town graduating from her own junior high. –SCOTT SILVERMAN

The way we know the kids are growing up: The bite marks are higher. –PHYLLIS DILLER

Yeah, I saw my parents today… It's all right, they didn't see me or anything. –MARGARET SMITH

My mom took me to a dog show and I won!! –RODNEY DANGERFIELD

When I was kidnapped, my parents snapped into action. They rented out my room. –WOODY ALLEN

My younger brother, Scott, he is kind of a criminal and I kind of blame myself 'cause I got him in a lot of trouble when we were kids. Anything I dared him to do he did. One time we were in the park, I dared him to steal this woman's purse and he did and the cops got him and took him down to the station and put him in the lineup with these other guys. Scott isn't very smart. They say, "First face to the right, then face to the left, then look straight ahead." And he's like, "That's her!" –TOM ARNOLD

In 1969, I was six years old. My father joined Nation of Islam. Six years old. Suddenly there's no Christmas and we have to fast for a month.

–BOBBY SLAYTON

On her father: He was a gambler and an alcoholic. He was also very vain. So one day he gave up his vices to save up enough money for a hair transplant. Two days after the transplant was complete, he got drunk and on a $20 bet he shaved his head…. So I owe him $20. –MARGARET SMITH

I got the fortunate job of playing the widowed father of three kids on *Full House.* It was wonderful, a great gig until my own three-year-old daughter, my real one, smelled my TV baby on my clothes and thought I was cheating on her. –BOB SAGET

Fathers are the geniuses of the house. We're the geniuses of the house because only a person intelligent as we could fake such stupidity. –BILL COSBY

I can't sleep. I have insomnia. I had a nightmare last night. I had a terrible dream. I dreamt my parents came to visit me…. That's it. –CATHY LADMAN

Nothing in life is "fun for the whole family." –JERRY SEINFELD

Usually when you come out your parents want you to keep it secret. You know they wanna slowly tell their friends. I came out. I'd been on television. There was a big article in *Newsday* on Long Island where they live. The headline said, "Frank Maya from Babylon, Long Island, is gay." Now, my father's name is also Frank Maya.... –FRANK MAYA

My mom wanted to know why I don't come home for the holidays more often. I told her I can't get Delta Airlines to wait in the yard while I run in. –MARGARET SMITH

When you get married and have a kid, you can't do all those things you wanted to do as a young existentialist of 17 or 18, like kill yourself. –AL RAE

My mother calls at 5:30 in the morning. I'm not a dairy farm. I don't like phone calls before six in the morning.
–RICHARD LEWIS

On her mom, the psychoanalyst: It's weird that I have a parent who's a shrink. It's hard to think of my mom solving other people's problems when she's the root of all mine.
–CAROL LEIFER

I'm getting ready to be a parent. I just turned 30 and I'm tired of cutting the grass. –JEFF FOXWORTHY

Our parents got divorced when we were kids and it was kind of cool. We got to go to divorce court with them. It was like a game show. My mom won the house and car. We're all excited. My dad got some luggage. –TOM ARNOLD

An answering machine…is like the stupidest gift to give your parents. No one ever calls them except for their kids. My mother put the appropriate message on the machine: "Look. We're not here right now. If you'd like to leave a message, leave one. If you don't want to leave one, don't. We're not going to be making decisions for you anymore. So make up your own g - - damn mind. Thank you." –JUDY GOLD

My mom and dad are Devo. It's kind of a problem. It really is. They sit at home naked with Frisbees on their heads. It's kind of a problem. I love my parents. I love you guys. I mean it. I have no friends. I have no life. I live in a moped.
–BOB SAGET

On his mom: I always wanted to do comedy, but my mother was not in favor of it. She used to wake me up in the middle of the night, "Vy don't you get a job? Vy don't you become a lawyer, an accountant. Do something. Become a doctor. Vy do you have to become an actor and make yourself crazy?" Mom, why do you talk to me like that? We're not even Jewish. –HARVEY KORMAN

Maybe there is no actual place called hell. Maybe hell is just having to listen to our grandparents breathe through their nose when they are eating a sandwich. –JIM CARREY

On vanity license plates: I got mine for a dollar 'cause my dad made it. –MITCHELL WALKER

If you have kids, God bless you. You know the only thing more wonderful than having kids is not. –BRENT CUSHMAN

The way I look at it, if the kids are still alive when my husband comes home from work, then I've done my job.
–ROSEANNE

On Father's Day greeting cards: I hate this occasion; I can never find the right card because they are all too nice.
–MARGARET SMITH

Guy says, "What's the latest dope on Wall Street?" Other guy says, "My son!"

–HENNY YOUNGMAN

Those signs—that "Baby on Board" crap—doesn't it make you want to hit the car harder? –SUE KOLINSKY

I'm the oldest of five kids. My name is Ngaio. Then there's Igui, Ishisoko, Iliasha, Jamilia. My mother's name is Orelia. My father's name is James—we're going to kick his ass.
–NGAIO BEALUM

People come up to me and they're worried…that I'll reproduce. –EMO PHILIPS

By the time my parents had me, they were old. My mother had labor pains and hot flashes. I was the only baby in the nursery wearing Depends. –MARIETTA DANIEL

I've got three kids. I had one with the birth control pill, one with a diaphragm, and another with the IUD. I don't know what happened to my IUD, but I have my suspicions. That kid picks up HBO. –ROSEANNE

I married an Italian girl. I figure we are going to have Irish kids with really great tanning potential. –JOEY CALLAHAN

My real father is finally coming around. He was worried that I was gonna be gay 'cause when I was eight years old my mother put a plant in my room. Like I'd walk in and go, "Oh, my God! A plant! Bud me. I want to be a florist." –SCOTT SILVERMAN

When it's time for me to have kids, I'm going to go natural—no hair, no makeup. –MARGO BLACK

My family is half Irish and half Swedish. They're all alcoholics, but we're real quiet about it. –BRETT BUTLER

I just got back from a pleasure trip. I took my mother-in-law to the airport. –HENNY YOUNGMAN

On being a lesbian: You know my family always said no man would be good enough for me. –SUZY BERGER

I love my mom. She's an Irish cook—which means she can't. –JIM MCCUE

Kids are cute, but they got that honesty thing and there's no need for that. I'm in the bathroom taking a shower and my daughter walks in. "Gosh, Mom, I hope that when I grow up my breasts will be nice and long like yours." –ROSEANNE

My mother has gossip dyslexia. She has to talk in front of people's backs. –RICHARD LEWIS

We'd ask [my mother] what she wanted for her birthday. Every year she'd say the same thing, "What do I want for my birthday? I want you kids to get along. All I want is peace in this house." Well, we saved a lot of money on gifts. –JUDY GOLD

It wasn't easy telling my family that I'm gay. I made my carefully worded announcement at Thanksgiving. It was very Norman Rockwell. I said, "Mom, would you please pass the gravy to a homosexual?" She passed it to my father. A terrible scene followed. Just kidding, Dad. –BOB SMITH

My dad is big old heavy-set drunk white trash. That's my dad, baby. My dad is not real bright—bright, but not real bright. But I love the guy. We go into this trophy shop because my basketball team won second place. We were in this shop and there are trophies everywhere. There are shelves and shelves of trophies. My dad looks around and goes, "This guy is really good." –FRED WOLFE

Father's Day Cards as seen on The Late Show:
 "Dad, I'm still amazed that you did it with Mom!"
"Happy Father's Day, and forget all that stuff I said on *Oprah*."
"Hey Fatty, easy on the fries. Love, Chelsea."

I wanted to do something nice so I bought my mother-in-law a chair. Now they won't let me plug it in. –HENNY YOUNGMAN

I was raised by just my mom. See, my father died when I was eight years old. At least, that's what he told us in the letter. –DREW CAREY

My grandfather's a little forgetful, but he likes to give me advice. One day, he took me aside and left me there.
–RON RICHARDS

I have nephews. I go visit my nephews. I get out of the car. They see me and drop what they are doing and hug my legs. I feel like the most important person on God's earth. Seven minutes later I would trade their pelts for whiskey. I look down at them. "How could you be so obnoxious!?" Then I look at my brother. –BRENT CUSHMAN

He was an angry man, Uncle Swanny. He had printed on his grave: "What are you lookin' at?" –MARGARET SMITH

I'm kinda depressed right now cuz we hadda put my grand-father in a rest home. Well, not actually—we didn't have the money. So we drove down the Turnpike…and put him in the rest area. –RICH VOS

My sister is a slut…. She has this little ritual. She does this every morning. She gets up. She checks the mail so she can find the address, calls a cab, and gets herself the hell home. –BONNIE MCFARLANE

My Aunt Sylvie came over for my parents' anniversary party. Her husband died 30 years ago and she can't get over it. She turns everything he owned into something. She was like, "So what do you think of this necklace? It's Dave's belt buckle." Then she said, "What do you think of these round ball earrings?" I'm like, "I don't even want to know, okay." –JUDY GOLD

> **…and always remember the last words of my grandfather, who said, "A truck!"**
>
> –EMO PHILIPS

This is my first day of mourning. My cousin died. He was a dyslexic policeman who had a heart attack. They found him by the phone trying to dial 119. –JOAN RIVERS

My unemployed brother-in-law gave up his job because of ill-ness. His boss got sick of him. –HENNY YOUNGMAN

Last month, my aunt passed away. She was cremated. We think that's what did it. –JONATHAN KATZ

On politically correct toys: I have new-age friends in California that try to do that kind of stuff and so they gave their little girl a toolbox of plastic tools. They were horrified later that night when they came into her room and found out she was putting the hammer to bed. –ROB BECKER

On his dad: He got his degree in embalming…. When we were little and we'd be getting dressed to go to church on Sundays, Dad would have me lay down on the table to tie my tie. –KILLER BEAZ

I'd like to have kids. I get those maternal feelings. Like when I'm laying on the couch and I can't reach the remote control. –KATHLEEN MADIGAN

I come from a typical American family. You know, me, my mother, her third husband, his daughter from a second marriage. My stepsister. Her illegitimate son. –CAROL HENRY

Now Mom's reached the point in her life where she doesn't care what people think. She has a bumper sticker on her car that says: "Honk, if your husband's watching TV and your oldest son doesn't know what he's doing, the other two are in California and New York, one's gay, your daughter's divorced, and you forgot to buy milk while at the store."

–BOB SMITH

P.C. Ew!

America is one of
the finest countries anyone ever stole.
–BOBCAT GOLDTHWAIT

Sometimes I think war is God's way of teaching us geography. –Paul Rodriguez

Is there anyone out there I haven't offended? –Mort Sahl

One day Little Red Riding Hood—who, although she wore red, was not affiliated with any gang—was walking through the woods with a basket of goodies for her grandmother when she met a homeless wolf who had been abused as a cub. –John Wing

There are no more car thieves. These are non-traditional commuters. Homeless people are full-time outdoorsmen. Prostitutes are sexual maintenance partners. –Paul Rodriguez

Religion

I think we should all treat each other like Christians. I, however, will not be responsible for the consequences. –George Carlin

I don't need to be born again. I got it right the first time. –Dennis Miller

Probably the worst thing about being Jewish during the Christmas-time holidays is shopping in stores, because the lines are so long. They should have a Jewish express line. "Look, I'm a Jew, it's not a gift. It's just paper towels." –Sue Kolinsky

On good vacation spots: Cardinal O'Connor says all gay activists are going to hell. So sometimes, when Harriet and I are sitting around wondering where to go on vacation, we think, well, hell would be nice. –Sara Cytron

Epitaph of an atheist: All dressed up but nowhere to go!
–THE ATOMIC CAFE

The Vatican is against surrogate mothers. Good thing they didn't have that rule when Jesus was born. –ELAYNE BOOSLER

The pro-life people. I have a problem with them. I say they should get a life 'cause if they had one, they'd leave everybody alone. –SUE KOLINSKY

On David Koresh: He thinks he's Jesus and I don't believe it, because there can't be three of us. –AL RAE

> **The only difference between Catholics and Jews is Jews are born with guilt and Catholics have to go learn it in school.**
>
> **–ELAYNE BOOSLER**

On Israel: It's not filled with your typical Jews that you know, the let-me-fill-out-your-tax-form Jews. It's more the will-you-hold-my-machine-gun-while-I-take-a-leak Jews. It's a different breed. –JON STEWART

The atheists have produced a Christmas play. It's called *Coincidence on 34th Street*. –JAY LENO

I was raised Catholic and received the Body and Blood of Christ every Sunday at Communion until the age of 30, when I became a vegetarian. –JOE QUEENAN

Ever say something and wish you could take it back? "Yeah, I'm a Jew. What are you skinheads going to do about it?"
–GREGG ROGELL

I don't go to church no more. It's getting too expensive. Too many plates, man. They pass 18 plates. I pull out a plate for myself. Pass it over here. I need some help. –EARTHQUAKE

We have amazing holidays. Yom Kippur—Jewish day of atonement. You don't eat for one day. All your sins for the year are wiped clean. Beat that with your little Lent. What is that? Forty days of absolution? Forty days to one. Even in sin you are paying retail. Wake up! Argue with the Man. –JON STEWART

I think most people believe in God...just in case. I don't want to be one of those people that says, "Hey, come on. There's no God. Aggghh!" and die and have to go, "Is there some sort of community service I can do?" –MARC MARON

I grew up Catholic, which is good. It gives you something to work out the rest of your life. –STEVE SWEENEY

I'm from a large Irish Catholic family. Large Irish Catholic. It's kind of redundant. –JOHN MCGIVERN

> I'm a member of the Jewish Community Center here in San Francisco. I don't really give a damn about Judaism. They've just got a great basketball court.
>
> –JOHNNY STEELE

I'm Jewish. I don't really follow the religion. Last time I was in temple, I was 13. I made my two grand. I got out of the business –MARK COHEN

Jews and Christians are different in a lot of ways. Some Christian people will actually have religious bumper stickers on their cars. Like "Jesus Is King." "The Lord Saves." Jews don't do that. You'll never see, "Honk If You Love Moses."
–GREGG ROGELL

I went to confession…. I said, "Father I want to hold men down and I want to whip them, I want to force them to caress my naked body." "Say 10 Hail Marys and meet me behind the Exxon station." –JOANNE DEARING

It's the little things in life that make us happy. Like watching a child on a swing. Listening to birds in the trees. Seeing a Hare Krishna get French-kissed by an air hammer.
–JUDY TENUTA

What do those people do? Do Krishnas go to the barber and say, "Hey, leave a little on the top?" –ROBIN WILLIAMS

I never suffered from any racism being Jewish. When I was a kid, once another kid made a racial slur and I told my dad about it. I'll never forget what my dad told me. He said, "Gregg, it doesn't matter what race you are or the color of your skin. There will always be some people out there who aren't gonna like you 'cause you're irritating."
–GREGG ROGELL

Sixty-six percent of Catholics have had sex at least once a week; the number would have been lower, but they factored in the priests. –DENNIS MILLER

I know you all pay your tithes, your 10 percent. I'll give God his money when I see him, and if he asks me why I was holding on to it, I'll say that there was a lot of false prophets on earth. I didn't know who "had your back." I ain't gonna give the money to the wrong man and still owe you when I got up here. If I'm going to hell, I'm gonna need that money for air conditioning. –EARTHQUAKE

If you want to be a holy man, you have to be committed. When you make a decision you cannot waver in any way. You'd never see Gandhi during a hunger strike sneaking into the kitchen in the middle of the night. "Gandhi...What are you doing down there?" "I, um, I thought I heard a prowler...and was going to hit him over the head with this giant bowl of potato salad." –JIM CARREY

I couldn't throw a ball. There's a problem you see in an Irish Catholic family. The boy that can't throw the ball is going to be the priest. –JOHN MCGIVERN

I grew up Catholic. To me, going to church was always really boring. I never liked it. But I went to a Catholic grammar school. You know what the nuns would tell me? "You know, Jim, the mass is a celebration. What does that tell you, young man?" It tells me that the Catholics don't know how to throw a frigging party. –JIMMY DORE

I found a letter I wrote to Santa Claus when I was a little kid that my mom saved. It was kind of cute. I'll read it to you. "Dear Santa, I'm not writing this letter to ask you for any toys. I know you won't give me any because I'm a Jew. Your apparent lack of compassion to the Jewish community is only a reflection of your racist policy of non-recognition toward the state of Israel.... I hope your sled gets clipped by a DC-10, you crash in the Andes Mountains, and you have to eat your reindeer to survive, you fat Nazi bastard." –GREGG ROGELL

My best friend is Lutheran and she told me that when Jesus was born, the Three Wise Men came to visit and brought frankincense and myrrh. Myrrh? To a baby shower?...I guess Mary was very polite about it, "Oh, myrrh, how lovely. One can never get enough myrrh..." –CATHY LADMAN

> **My husband and I had a really nice wedding. We have a mixed marriage. I'm Jewish and he ain't. For my family, he crushed a beer can under his foot. For his family, I pretended I was a virgin.**
>
> –ROSEANNE

I was raised in the Jewish tradition, taught never to marry a gentile woman, shave on Saturday, and more especially never to shave a gentile woman on Saturday. –WOODY ALLEN

TV evangelists aren't holy men—they're just ambitious. I saw one guy who was so ambitious he actually became jealous of the Lord. You could tell halfway through his sermon when he said, "When I was a child, I wanted to be the savior of the world. Then they told me that Jesus was the son of God and I realized, it's all in who you know." –JIM CARREY

I learned something the other day. I learned that Jehovah's Witnesses do not celebrate Halloween. I guess they don't like strangers going up to their door and annoying them. –BRUCE CLARK

Pope John Paul said Easter Mass in 57 different languages, and that was just for New York City cab drivers. –DAVID LETTERMAN

Is it blasphemy if when you die, you have your crotch cremated and spread over the Virgin Islands? –BRUCE BAUM

Priests are very much against condoms…'cause they are getting caught in altar boys' braces. –JOHNNY STEELE

I'm Jewish. People hate Jews. People think we have all the money. They think you see another Jew and he gives you free s - - t. Go to a car dealership. Goldberg Chevrolet. "Are you Jewish?" "Yeah." "Take the car. Don't tell the Christians. See you at the meeting. See any Messiahs? Call us." Everybody hates the Jews. But when you need a lawyer, it's, "Get me a Jew! I want to be surrounded by Jews. A Leibowitz, a Hoffman and Feldman." –MARK UNGER

The Pope. Great guy. But in a fashion sense, he's one hat away from being the Grand Wizard of the Klu Klux Klan.

–JON STEWART

Millions who long for immortality don't know what to do on a rainy Sunday afternoon. –SUSAN ERTZ

On television preachers: They say they don't favor any particular denomination, but I think we've all seen their eyes light up at tens and twenties. –DENNIS MILLER

Jehovah's Witnesses believe only 144,00 people will enter heaven. There are almost two million Jehovah's Witnesses in this country…talk about overbooking a flight.
–WAYNE TURMEL

Can't We All Just Get Along?

You know, it's easy to be politically correct and a liberal when you live in a gated community. –BOBCAT GOLDTHWAIT

I like hip hop. I'm working with Ice Cube and Ice-T, Herb Tea, Tupak and his cousin Chicken Pox. I'm changing my name to Snapple. –PAUL MOONEY

What's the difference between a gay comic and a straight comic? Nothing! –WHOOPI GOLDBERG

Usually I perform for straight audiences and it's kind of fun because they assume that I'm straight until I start talking— then they're like "wait a minute, I know that accent."
–SCOTT SILVERMAN

I hate when people look back on the good old days. When they say: "Wasn't it great back in the fifties?" Like that was a great time. Yeah, remember when black people and white people couldn't go to school together? Those were the halcyon days. –MARK FARRELL

I'm originally from Cuba. I live in Miami now. What a shocker, huh? Who could have guessed? Outside of Florida, people have no idea of what a Cuban is. Most Americans think Cubans are Mexicans with belts. –AL ROMERO

You know, the good thing about gangs is they carpool.
–JOHN MENDOZA

I'd like to have kids one day. I want to be called "Mommie" by someone other than the Spanish guys on the streets.
–CAROL LEIFER

At PBS, they've announced that they're doing a Hispanic version of *Sesame Street*. In the first episode, [Governor] Pete Wilson shows up and denies services to Bert and Ernie.
–BILL MAHER

There's a stereotype that black people are lazy. I don't know if that's true, but I know white people went all the way to Africa to get out of doing work. –LANCE CROUTHER

> **People come up to me and talk after shows to share their experiences. One guy once said to me, "Well, I'm straight, but I've had a homosexual experience." I'm like, "Exactly what did you do? Buy a pair of shoes and a belt that matched?"**
>
> –SCOTT SILVERMAN

I got another friend. He's half Polish, half Jewish. He's a janitor, but he owns the building. –JACKIE MASON

I never believed in Santa Claus because I knew no white dude would come into my neighborhood after dark.
–DICK GREGORY

I'm in the market today and a guy runs up behind me and says, "The majority of people who say they are deaf are faking it." I said, "Hey pal, I'm going to pretend that I didn't hear that." –BRUCE BAUM

On the Gay Pride parade: They always give my stepfather a sign. The last one said: "My son is gay and that's okay." He didn't think that was enthusiastic enough. He scrambled the sign and rewrote it so it said: "My son's a queen and that's peachy keen." –SCOTT SILVERMAN

I don't understand why gay people want to be in the military …'cause they only get one outfit to wear. –KEVIN MAYE

Yes, of course I am half Italian and half Polish. So I'm always putting a hit out on myself! –JUDY TENUTA

Terrorists never take black hostages. You know why terrorists never take black hostages, don't you? 'Cause we're bad bargaining chips. –DAVE CHAPPELLE

I wish blacks owned more stuff. Like I wish we had our own airline. Wouldn't that be great? The boarding announcements would be really different than the ones you have now. Instead of, "Flight 512, now boarding for Gate 17." It would be, "Uhhh, excuse me….But if you bought a ticket to Detroit, I suggest you get the hell on the plane….We leaving." –MARSHA WARFIELD

I'm an ethnic American and so are all of you. That's what made America the greatest country in the world. A true melting pot. I say, where else but in America could a Mexican girl date a white guy, drive a Japanese car, go to a Chinese restaurant, and come back and be arrested by a black cop. –PAUL RODRIGUEZ

I've heard comics say if you don't speak American language you should get out of here. Really, yeah, you don't sound like you're from here, Navaho. –BOBCAT GOLDTHWAIT

I had a club foot and I had a brace…I walked with a limp. Thank God I lived in the ghetto. The people that didn't know

me thought I was cool. "Hey, check out this brother's walk."
–DAMON WAYANS

Now I live in Greenwich Village. It's so gay you can't get a straight answer. The one nice thing about it is when a guy says he just wants to be friends, he's serious. –EMMY GAY

You now how black humor got started? It started on slave ships. Cat was rowing and dude says, "What you laughing about?" He said, "Yesterday I was king." –RICHARD PRYOR

Let me make sure I'm crystal clear on this issue: Heavy metal fans are buying heavy metal records, taking the records home and listening to the records and then blowing their heads off with shotguns. Where's the problem?
–DENIS LEARY

I like black people…. The only thing I don't like is when black people come to a show, sit right down in front, and suck up all the light. –MARSHA WARFIELD

A lady came up to me on the street and pointed at my suede jacket. "You know a cow was murdered for that jacket?" she sneered. I replied in a psychotic tone, "I didn't know there were any witnesses. Now I'll have to kill you too."
–JAKE JOHANSEN

Cold weather makes it very nice for race relations. Last month, when it was 15 below zero, I walked out of nightclub. A drunk walked up to me and said, "Why don't you go back to Africa…and take me with you." –DICK GREGORY

I'm on the Irish liquid diet. Slimfast and Bailey's. Three shakes a day and you're ready for the Betty Ford Center and a liver transplant. –KEVIN MEANEY

Native Americans are angry over the historical inaccuracies of the movie *Pocahontas*. Apparently, the real Pocahontas was much younger, much shorter, and rarely sang duets with her cartoon husband. –CONAN O'BRIEN

> I no longer believe it is right and proper for us to wear fur...because it's summer for Christ's sake. I have mine in storage.
>
> –ROSEANNE

I used to play cowboys and Indians. I was always one of the Indians. I had my own casino. –BRIAN KILEY

You get your penis severed. Here is a one in a million opportunity to get something better attached. I'd be phoning the morgue—in Compton. –PAUL RODRIGUEZ

My best friend is a guy half Italian, half Jewish. If he can't buy it wholesale, he steals it. –JACKIE MASON

Growing up in New York, you automatically take Spanish. You figure Puerto Ricans speak Spanish, how tough could it be? –BOBBY SLAYTON

Your mother is so black, everytime she goes to night school, the teacher marks her absent. –DAMON WAYANS

Rambo is a fantasy. I was in Vietnam. I didn't see no Rambo. I saw a bunch of Sambos on that frontline. –PAUL MOONEY

My parents were worried about me getting married.... So I got married. But they have one problem with it...she's black.... But she's a doctor so that's okay. –MARLA LUKOFSKY

Remember the scene in *West Side Story* when a guy is running through Spanish Harlem yelling out, "Maria" and only one woman comes to the window? –BOBBY SLAYTON

You say there are no Oriental blacks. If not, who gave them the idea to make those big radios? –GEORGE WALLACE

I'm glad we had a Miss America named Vanessa, though. I was tired of people named Becky Sue, Nancy, and s - - t. We had a Vanessa. It's almost like having a president named Darnell. –MARSHA WARFIELD

Clarence Thomas and Anita Hill. Black-on-black crime at the highest level. Cause you know Clarence pinched that ass. He's married to a white woman—no ass at home.
–EDDIE GRIFFIN

If ever you see me getting beaten by the police, put down the video camera and come help me.

–BOBCAT GOLDTHWAIT

Men look at me and think I'm going to walk on their backs or something. The only time I'll walk on your back is if there's something on the other side of you I want.
–MARGARET CHO

On Mexicans: We're afraid of mandatory busing because we know the minute you get all the Chicanos on the bus, we're not going to school. –PAUL RODRIGUEZ

I got another friend. Half German. Half Polish. Hates Jews. Can't remember why. –JACKIE MASON

On the Menendez brothers jury: You can't come up with a verdict. Try this: Close your damn eyes and pretend they are black. There's your f - - king verdict. –THEA VIDALE

Black women, we have attitude. We are the only people on earth born knowing how to roll our eyes with them closed. –MARSHA WARFIELD

Don't hoo, hoo, hoo me. There's a fine line between hoo, hoo, hoo and heil, heil, heil. –BOBCAT GOLDTHWAIT

According to a new study from Italy, some women are actually able to hear with their breasts. Of course this is great for Italian men, because they talk with their hands. –JAY LENO

Yeah, I'm a Mexican. Just like the kind that piss you off on the freeway…we're going 35 miles an hour. That's 'cause we've got 40 Mexicans in the trunk. –PAUL RODRIGUEZ

I'm half Irish, half Colombian. I don't know whether to have a beer or do a line of cocaine at a family gathering. –BECKY DONOHUE

Japanese Prime Minister Tomiichi Murayama apologized for Japan's part in World War II…. However, he still hasn't mentioned anything about karaoke. –DAVID LETTERMAN

I wish I could control show business for a while. I wish I could produce shows, make the kind of shows I want. I'd have a movie, a remake with Meryl Streep and Robert Redford called *Get Out of Africa.* –MARSHA WARFIELD

To the Beltway and Beyond!

*I'll admit it—I didn't vote.
I didn't like any of those bastards
enough to risk jury duty.*
–Christopher Case

Ninety-eight percent of the adults in this country are decent, hard-working, honest Americans. It's the other lousy two percent that gets all the publicity. But then, we elected them.
–LILY TOMLIN

Scientists believe that monkeys can be taught to think, lie, and even play politics within their community. If we can just teach them to cheat on their wives we can save millions on congressional salaries. –JAY LENO

The reason there are two senators for each state is so that one can be the designated driver. –JAY LENO

We're a trillion dollars in debt. Who do we owe this money to? Someone named Vinnie? –ROBIN WILLIAMS

The American government is making nuclear weapons like there is no tomorrow. –EMO PHILIPS

Put a federal agency in change of the Sahara Desert and it would run out of sand. –PEGGY NOONAN

A child can go only so far in life without potty training. It is not mere coincidence that six of the last seven presidents were potty trained, not to mention nearly half of the nation's state legislators.

–DAVE BARRY

I looked up "politics" in the dictionary and it's actually a combination of two words: "poli" which means many and "tics" which means bloodsuckers. –JAY LENO

A conservative is a man who is too cowardly to fight and too fat to run. –ELBERT HUBBARD

If life were fair, Dan Quayle would be making a living asking, "Do you want fries with that?" –JOHN CLEESE

I owe the government $3,400 in taxes. So I sent them two hammers and a toilet seat. –MICHAEL MCSHANE

> **Chief Justice William Rehnquist had back surgery that kept him away from Supreme Court duties. It had to be fixed. The problem was so bad it had caused the entire court to lean to the far right.**
>
> –PAUL RYAN

I don't know what senator will be getting Bob Packwood's old office, but here's a little bit of advice: Hose down the desk and steam clean the carpet with Lysol. –JAY LENO

It seems ironic that the Republican party is always telling voters that they will "clean house." I thought that Republicans usually hire illegal aliens for that task. –ELBERT HUBBARD

On Oliver North giving testimony: He couldn't answer a personal question about his own life without leaning over to that counsel guy. I kept wanting to say to that lawyer, "If you give him the answers, how will he learn?" –PAULA POUNDSTONE

Heidi Fleiss has a point. You know what happens to a woman who is arrested for prostitution? She goes to jail. You know what happens to a man? He gets re-elected. –JAY LENO

On Oliver North's testimony: Do you think Gordon Liddy's sitting at home going, "If only I had a uniform..." –ROBIN WILLIAMS

Times Books is publishing the Bob Packwood diaries. They are putting out an audiotape version. They'll use Senator Packwood's actual voice. In fact, they say it's so realistic, that you can almost feel his tongue sticking in your ear. –JAY LENO

Democracy means that anyone can grow up to be president and anyone who doesn't grow up can be vice president. –JOHNNY CARSON

The Iowa straw poll ended in a dead heat between Bob Dole and Phil Gramm. Fortunately they didn't use a wet T-shirt contest as a tiebreaker. –WILL DURST

A Congresswoman from Utah is going to have a baby next September. She will be the first member of Congress to breastfeed since Bob Packwood. –CONAN O'BRIEN

They want to put Reagan's head on Mount Rushmore. A couple of snags in the plan. They're not sure that granite is a dense enough material to accurately portray the former president's head. –DENNIS MILLER

Former Alabama Governor George Wallace endorsed Bob Dole for president, which seems to indicate Detective Mark Fuhrman has decided not to run. It was so hard to understand his testimony from under that hood. –WILL DURST

On George Bush being the education president: Oh sure, lucky for us he's not the nutrition president. We'd all starve.
–JOY BEHAR

I began performing political comedy the same year Ronald Reagan began performing his. –KATE CLINTON

Yesterday the Senate ruled that the Packwood hearings will not be held in public. Out of habit, Packwood suggested, "We could go back to my place." –CONAN O'BRIEN

There's nothing wrong with Bob Dole that an hour with Divine Brown couldn't fix. –ERIC BOGOSIAN

On Pat Buchanan's speech at the 1992 GOP convention: It probably sounded better in the original German. –MOLLY IVINS

The Supreme Court has ruled that they cannot have a nativity scene in Washington, D.C. This wasn't for any religious reasons. They couldn't find three wise men and a virgin.
–JAY LENO

Mayor Giuliani kicked Yasser Arafat out of a private party at Lincoln Center. On his way out of the party, Arafat was heard saying, "Hey, I've blown up better places than this."
–BILL MAHER

Do you think Clinton would have stayed in D.C. if it had been the Million Woman March? –WILL DURST

They had the 95th running of the Boston Marathon recently. This year the people racing in the event had two routes to choose from: the traditional route or a dozen laps around Ted Kennedy. –DAVID LETTERMAN

Washington Mayor Marion Barry is going on a trip to Africa. He says he wants to find his roots and smoke some of them. –BILL MAHER

To pay for his tax cuts President Clinton is still trying to turn a number of governmental agencies into private corporations. Well, this shouldn't be too hard. Clinton already proved he can turn a number of Democrat incumbents into private citizens last election. –DENNIS MILLER

I think there are three basic questions being raised by the Whitewater hearings now: What did President Clinton know, when did he know it, and who was he dating at the time? –JEFF ALTMAN

> **When Marion Barry was off and running for mayor, he had a new campaign slogan: "I'll get drugs off the street—one gram at a time."**
>
> –BILL MAHER

I voted for the Democrats because I didn't like the way the Republicans were running the country. Which is turning out to be like shooting yourself in the head to stop your headache. –JACK MAYBERRY

On Arkansas: Employment went up when two people got a job. –JACKIE MASON

The forces in the White House want Hillary to tone down? From what? Did I miss her crazed-leather-biker-chick period? –BEVERLY MICKINS

It was Hillary Clinton's turn to be surrounded by adoring females in Beijing where she attended the fourth International Conference on Women. No report that she brought back any samples for Bill. –WILL DURST

It doesn't take long to figure out that in that town [Washington, D.C.] we don't have our priorities in order. Two men can now kiss in the White House, but you can't even smoke. –MICKEY DEAN

Chicago is busy sweeping prostitutes from their streets in anticipation of next year's Democratic Convention. So what do you think: They worried about competition or professional jealousy?

–WILL DURST

Congressman Mel Reynolds has been convicted of having sex with a 16-year-old. He told her not to tell anybody, but apparently it slipped out at a pep rally. –GARRY SHANDLING

Clinton's reelection committee so far in 10 weeks has raised almost $10 million—and that's just from the kissing booth. –BILL MAHER

Al Gore turned down a chance to be on *The Simpsons*. He explained, "I've never been animated and I'm not going to start now." –CONAN O'BRIEN

I keep having this dream with me and Ross Perot in bed and he keeps going, "Let me finish…" –ROBIN WILLIAMS

Bob Dole accused President Clinton of pushing too much, too hard, too quickly. Oh, I'm sorry...that was Paula Jones.
–CONAN O'BRIEN

At a town meeting in Rhode Island, President Clinton said that there are powerful forces threatening to bring down his administration. Yeah, I think they are called hormones.
–JAY LENO

It turns out that back in 1980, Hillary Clinton invested in sugar, hogs, and cattle. She got the idea from watching her husband eat breakfast. –CONAN O'BRIEN

President Clinton celebrated his 19th wedding anniversary this year. Bill said he celebrated with a romantic dinner for two and a night in a fancy hotel. Hillary said she just saw a movie. –JON STEWART

The Kennedy compound in Palm Beach has been sold. The new owner said he plans to move in as soon as they clean out the empties. –CONAN O'BRIEN

Random Acts of Silliness

I'm desperately trying to figure out why kamikaze pilots wore helmets.
−Dave Edison

My grandfather invented Cliff's Notes. It all started back in 1912.... Well, to make a long story short... –STEVEN WRIGHT

I have the brain of a German shepherd and the body of a sixteen-year-old boy. They're out in my car and I'd like you to see them right now. –BOB SAGET

I was an accountant. I wasn't a very good accountant. I always felt that if you got within two or three bucks of it that was close enough. –BOB NEWHART

Why isn't "phonetic" spelled the way it sounds? –THE ATOMIC CAFE

I got an "A" in philosophy because I proved my professor didn't exist. –JUDY TENUTA

You know what's great about coffee? It's the only meal for which the name of the food is also the official name of the event: coffee. "We'll get together for coffee." We don't know what we're doing, but we know what we'll be having—coffee. No one ever talks about getting together for lamb, or Fresca, or grapes. You never hear it because it doesn't quite have the same draw as coffee. –PAUL REISER

I'm so insecure, I'm not sure I'm insecure. I worry so much, sometimes I worry...that I don't worry enough. –TIM HALPERN

I used to work at International House of Pancakes. You set your goals. You go for them. It's a dream. I made it happen. It was the worst job I ever had in my entire life. I tell you something: When people would be rude...I'd touch their eggs. –PAULA POUNDSTONE

I'm a comedian and I'm supposed to tell you s - - t. If I didn't tell you anything I'd be a mime. –BARRY DIAMOND

I got in a fight one time with a really big guy and he said, "I'm going to mop the floor with your face." I said, "You'll be sorry." He said, "Oh yeah? Why?" and I said, "Well, you won't be able to get into the corners very well." –EMO PHILIPS

> I guess I just prefer to see the dark side of things. The glass is always half empty. And cracked. And I just cut my lip on it. And chipped a tooth.
>
> –JANEANE GAROFALO

I'm writing an unauthorized autobiography. –STEVEN WRIGHT

All the big corporations depreciate their possessions, and you can, too, provided you use them for business purposes. For example, if you subscribe to the *Wall Street Journal*, a business-related newspaper, you can deduct the cost of your house, because, in the words of U.S. Supreme Court Chief Justice Warren Burger in a landmark 1979 tax decision: "Where else are you going to read the paper? Outside? What if it rains?" –DAVE BARRY

What do prostitutes do at a convention when they let their hair down? Do they wear flat shoes and stand up a lot? –ROSEANNE

On the movie Annie: Tomorrow? No, little ugly b- - -h, we're killing you tonight. There be no tomorrow. –PAUL MOONEY

When I tell people I'm a comedian they say, "Oh, are you funny?" I say, "No, it's not that kind of comedy." –BETSY SALKIND

Anyone else ever just feel the fetal position coming on? –PAULA POUNDSTONE

Link between eating meat and war: You eat enough meat, you want to kill somebody. That's the way it works. –DENIS LEARY

She saw a sign saying "Wet Floor." So she did. –JOAN RIVERS

You don't know what C-section is?…It's this section over here. Great seats. –BOB SAGET

I was arrested for selling illegal-sized paper. –STEVEN WRIGHT

I would love to speak a foreign language but I can't. So I grew hair under my arms instead. –SUE KOLINSKY

Carpe per diem—Seize the check. –ROBIN WILLIAMS

I'm everything you were afraid your little girl would grow up to be—and your little boy. –BETTE MIDLER

I used to be a narrator for bad mimes. –STEVEN WRIGHT

Where lipstick is concerned, the important thing is not the color, but to accept God's final decision on where your lips end. –JERRY SEINFELD

If all the world's a stage, why do only half of us wear makeup? –BRAD STEIN

Let's all go someplace at once. Act like it's a complete coincidence. They're just having a rush. We don't even know each other. We're just looking at some frozen foods. Then one at a time, we each go up and buy a Slim Jim. Screw up their inventory. –PAULA POUNDSTONE

Curiosity killed the cat, but for a while I was the suspect.
–STEVEN WRIGHT

If only God would give me some clear sign. Like making a large deposit in my name in a Swiss bank. –WOODY ALLEN

People are stupid. Not us. Not us. I don't mean us. I'm talking about the others….Thank God they aren't here tonight.
–PAUL REISER

Happiness is the quiet lull between problems. –PAUL REISER'S FATHER

A truck full of chickens overturned on the Long Island Expressway. Hundreds of chickens crossed the road but no one has been able to figure out why. –NORM MACDONALD

If crime fighters fight crime, and firefighters fight fire, what do freedom fighters fight? They never mention that part to us, do they? –GEORGE CARLIN

Do you know how many polyesters died to make that shirt?
–STEVE MARTIN

On working at the International House of Pancakes: People all the time complained about the service. We weren't slow. The floors were sticky. –PAULA POUNDSTONE

After they make Styrofoam, what do they ship it in? –STEVEN WRIGHT

Clothes spend most of their lives waiting in the closet, in the hamper, in the drawer. There are shirts in your house going, "He never picks me." Laundry day is the only exciting day 'cause the washing machine is the nightclub of clothes. It's dark, bubbles happening, they are all kind of dancing around. The shirt grabs the underwear. "Come on, babe, let's go…" –JERRY SEINFELD

You know what I don't understand? I don't understand… Spanish. –HOWIE MANDEL

I. Magnin—it's a shotgun. –CAROL LEIFER

If all the nations in the world are in debt, where did all the money go? –STEVEN WRIGHT

I always wanted to be somebody, but I should have been more specific.

–LILY TOMLIN

I always loved comedy, but I never knew it was something you could learn to do. I always thought that some people are born comedians. Just like some people are born dentists. –PAUL REISER

If the pen is mightier than the sword, in a duel I'll let you have the pen! –STEVEN WRIGHT

Last night, I dreamed I ate a 10-pound marshmallow, and when I woke up, the pillow was gone. –TOMMY COOPER

I hate the outdoors. To me, the outdoors is where the car is.
–WILL DURST

Weather forecast for tonight: dark. –GEORGE CARLIN

What's another word for thesaurus? –STEVEN WRIGHT

I like it when I can go to a place like the supermarket as an adult and get something. When I don't want something I can put it back wherever I am in the supermarket because I don't work for the supermarket. I don't care if the store manager is looking right at me. "Yeah those are my peaches on the Pennzoil. What about it?' It's "impulse not-buying."
–JERRY SEINFELD

> ### I don't like movies. I like plays. This way, I can stand up and tell them it stinks.
>
> –LINDA HERSKOVIC

I own the erasers for all the miniature golf pencils. –STEVEN WRIGHT

Ever watch ants just crawling around? They walk in that single straight line, a long, long mile of ants. Sometimes they will walk over and pick up their dead friends and carry those around. I'm pretty sure it's because they can get in the carpool lane and pass up that line. –ELLEN DEGENERES

I always find money in public phones—when I bring a screwdriver along –LINDA HERSKOVIC

I hate it when my hair is engaged in unauthorized activities.
–PAULA POUNDSTONE

Basically, a tool is an object that enables you to take advantage of the laws of physics and mechanics in such a way that you can seriously injure yourself. –DAVE BARRY

Man invented language to satisfy his deep need to complain. –LILY TOMLIN

Comedy is tragedy plus time. –CAROL BURNETT

I had a lot of toys as a kid. The best toy is something you get on your own, like a cardboard box. Five years old, you get boxes like the ones refrigerators come in. When you are five years old, that's the closest you get to having your own apartment. –JERRY SEINFELD

I saw a subliminal advertising executive, but only for a second. –STEVEN WRIGHT

The problem with self improvement is knowing when to quit. –DAVID LEE ROTH

May the forces of evil be confused on the way to your house. –GEORGE CARLIN

I wrote a few children's books. Not on purpose. –STEVEN WRIGHT

Are tectonic plates dishwasher safe? –HERB CAEN

I'm a psychic amnesiac. I know in advance what I'll forget. –MICHAEL McSHANE

Last Halloween was bad for me. I got real beat up. I went to a party dressed as a piñata. –JIM SAMUELS

I don't even have a savings account because I don't know my mom's maiden name and apparently that's key to the whole thing there. I go in every few weeks and guess. –PAULA POUNDSTONE

Anywhere is walking distance if you've got the time.
–STEVEN WRIGHT

What if everything is an illusion and nothing exists? In that case, I definitely overpaid for my carpet. –WOODY ALLEN

I worry that the person who thought up Muzak may be thinking up something else. –LILY TOMLIN

In high school, I was voted the girl most likely to become a nun. That may not be impressive to you, but it was quite an accomplishment at the Hebrew Academy. –RITA RUDNER

Ever wonder if illiterate people get the full effect of alphabet soup? –JOHN MENDOZA

There will be a rain dance Friday night, weather permitting.
–GEORGE CARLIN

On underwear. I'm opening a pair of underwear the other day and a little piece of paper falls out right on the floor. I pick it up. "Inspected by Mary Lou." "Well, thank God," I thought, "That last pair burst into flames. Now that Mary Lou's on the job, I can walk around safe in my underwear."
–MARGARET SMITH

You know what's fun to do? Rent an adult movie, take it home, record over it with *The Wizard of Oz*, then return it so the next guy that rents it is thinking, "When is this Dorothy chick going to get naked?" –MARK PITTA

Why do the Yellow Pages advertise on television? We don't get a choice of which Yellow Pages we want. James Earl Jones, one of the finest actors in the world, has a commercial for New Jersey Bell Yellow Pages. It doesn't make sense. He actually says, "Nine out of 10 people use the New Jersey Yellow pages." What does the other jerk use? The Texas Yellow Pages? You know why nine out of 10 people use the Yellow Pages? Because the 10th person calls information—I'm that guy. –EDDIE BRILL

God sneezed. What could I say to Him? –HENNY YOUNGMAN

On fire drills: In elementary school, in case of fire you have to line up quietly in single-file line from smallest to tallest. What is the logic? Do tall people burn slower? –WARREN HUTCHERSON

> I don't mind hecklers. I know how to ignore people. I was an airline stewardess.
>
> –JOANNE DEARING

Ever notice how irons have a setting for "permanent" press? I don't get it... –STEVEN WRIGHT

I have a message from the National Pancake Institute. It says, "F - - k waffles." –GEORGE CARLIN

I studied psychology and agriculture at college. Which means I basically learned how to raise a pig's self-esteem. "What's the matter, pig? You're not eating your s - - t." –WINSTON SPEAR

I don't care about anything. Like yesterday, Jimmy cracked corn. I don't care. –HOWIE MANDEL

> Have you ever noticed the mannequins in the store have the natural look, the bra-less look. They have a sweater on with little points. Why would I buy a sweater that can't keep a mannequin warm?
>
> –ELAYNE BOOSLER

You can't have everything. Where would you put it?
–STEVEN WRIGHT

On breathable panty-shields: You want something breathing down your pants that doesn't pay rent? –ELAYNE BOOSLER

NyQuil—capital N, small y, big f - - kin' Q! I love that f - - kin' Q, don't you? What a great advertising idea—put a huge f - - kin' Q on the box. They'll get high and stare at it. "The Q is talkin' to me! The Q is talkin' to me!" –DENIS LEARY

Energy experts have announced the development of a new fuel made from human brain tissue. It's called assohol.
–GEORGE CARLIN

Let me ask you something—if someone's lying, are their pants really on fire? –JERRY SEINFELD

Encyclopedia is a Latin term. It means to paraphrase a term paper. –GREG RAY

I promised some people I'd water their plants and take care of their animals while they went on vacation. They're farmers. –JANINE DITULLIO

On receiving a salad shooter: What was I supposed to do? Walk into a bar and hold up a vegetarian? –CAROL HENRY

On high school reunions: Don't go if you've never gone. You get that letter in the mail. You feel like you only have six months to make something of yourself. –DREW CAREY

Sex

Sex without love is an empty experience. But as empty experiences go, it's one of the best.
–WOODY ALLEN

I'm Catholic…My mother and I were unpacking and she found my diaphragm. I had to tell her it was a bathing cap for my cat. –LIZZ WINSTEAD

On Dr. Ruth: She came up to me and said, "Judy, I'm a sex therapist." Yeah, well, I would be too if I came up to everyone's belt buckle. –JUDY TENUTA

My mother is Welsh, my father is Hungarian—which makes me Wel-Hung. –BILLY RIBACK

We have reason to believe that man first walked upright to free his hands for masturbation. –LILY TOMLIN

Masturbation, don't knock it. It's sex with someone you love. –WOODY ALLEN

I lost my job. No, I really didn't lose my job. I know where my job is, still. It's just when I got there, there's this new guy doing it…. I lost my girl. No, I didn't really lose my girl. I know where my girl is, still. It's just when I got there, there's this new guy doing it. –BOBCAT GOLDTHWAIT

I read books that say if you want to keep sex hot you tell a person what you want. How do you tell 'em you want somebody else? –ELAYNE BOOSLER

I do this Jewish foreplay kind of thing. I want you. Take me. Lick me. Suck me. I love you. I want you. I'm your slave. You're my slave. Then I go, "What do you have? What is that, a little boil behind your neck?" –RICHARD LEWIS

I tell ya, sex is getting harder all the time. Me and my wife were trying to have sex for hours last night and finally gave up. I asked her, "What, you can't think of anybody either?" –RODNEY DANGERFIELD

I'm too shy to express my sexual needs except over the phone to people I don't know. –GARRY SHANDLING

On masturbation: Shaking hands with the unemployed.
–GEORGE CARLIN

I was pretty old when I had my first sexual experience. The reason was that I was born by cesarean section and had no frame of reference. –JEFF HILTON

Magic Johnson admits that he was sexually promiscuous, got the HIV virus and possibly infected half the women he was with. And we call him a hero. Pee Wee Herman was in a theater, by himself, practicing safe sex... –MARSHA WARFIELD

You ever heard of Freud Airlines? They have two sections— guilt and non-guilt.... The seats go all the way back to childhood. –ELLEN ORCHID

I slept with a French girl once. It wasn't magical, it wasn't mystical, and it wasn't worth the five bucks. –TONY MOREWOOD

I'm so HIV paranoid I can't even watch VH-1 –MARC PRICE

Shopping is better than sex. If you're not satisfied after shopping you can make an exchange for something you really like. –ADRIENNE GUSOFF

Women have more than one orgasm. Two orgasms. Multiple orgasms. I'll believe it when I see it. Men have two orgasms. One with the woman and one when we are telling our buddies about it. –GARRY SHANDLING

In the new sex survey they found that 8 percent of people had sex four or more times a week. Now here's the interesting part. That number drops to 2 percent when you add the phrase, "With partner." –DAVID LETTERMAN

The 1950s was the most sexually frustrated decade ever. Ten years of foreplay. –LILY TOMLIN

I'm so paranoid I'm afraid I'll get AIDS from masturbation. So I'm not masturbating anymore until I get to know myself better.

–TIM HALPERN

Everybody should practice safe sex. 'Cause nobody wants to be doing it and put an eye out. –EMMY GAY

Sex is scary. What is sex going to be in the '90s? You and you. That's right. Come home, put on that music that you like, "I only have eyes for me." You don't have to fake an orgasm anymore. 'Cause if it's bad, who's gonna tell it's you? –ROBIN WILLIAMS

My sex life is like shootin' pool with a rope! –RODNEY DANGERFIELD

I tried phone sex. I'm a hypochondriac. I got an ear infection. –RICHARD LEWIS

People know that I talk about this condom case that I carry with me everywhere. It's a three-condom case. You know, you have one for every occasion. What a lot of people don't know is that this thing comes in a six-pack, an eight-pack, and the 12-pack. The six-pack—that's for Hispanic brothers making love Monday, Tuesday, Wednesday, Thursday, Friday, Saturday, but off on Sunday. The eight-pack—that's for the black brothers for making love on Monday, Tuesday, Wednesday, Thursday, Friday, Saturday, and twice on Sunday. The 12-pack—that's for the white cats: January, February, March.... –MICHAEL COLYAR

It's really hard with lesbian relationships to know when your anniversary date is. Is it your first date? The first time you go to bed together? Is it the day you move in? Lucky for my girlfriend and me, all those things happened at the same time. –LYNDA MONTGOMERY

In Australia, they have a big whorehouse that sold shares and went public. The first day on the market, they say the stock went up and down and up and down. –BILL MAHER

Some people say, "Gee, well, making love and wearing a condom is like taking a shower and wearing a raincoat." Maybe, but these days, making love and not wearing a raincoat is like taking a shower and wearing a toaster. –MARC PRICE

I used to play doctor with this little girl in my neighborhood all the time. One time we got caught. Luckily, it was a Wednesday and we were just playing golf. –BRIAN KILEY

I met a guy the other night, I went home with him, I was going to have sex with him that night, but at the last minute I thought better of it. But I wound up staying over anyway. The next morning I changed my mind and had sex with him in the morning, which was nice and all, but then I spent the whole day wondering if he would respect me in the evening. –LYNN HARRIS

I don't think with my dick, my dick thinks for me. –FRANKLIN

Yesterday in Egypt, archeologists discovered the burial site of the 50 children of Ramses II.... Fifty children! What I want to know is, who decided to name a condom after this guy? –CONAN O'BRIEN

I went to the gynecologist. She goes, "God, you're clean. You are so clean. How do you stay so clean?" I said, "It's easy. I have a woman come in twice a week." –KAREN RIPLEY

> ## If men could control their dicks, you think that we would let them wake up every morning hard?
>
> –FRANKLIN

On sex in the kitchen: Nothing like a little stove top stuffing. –TONY EDWARDS

A man in Ohio was arrested and when the police searched him they found he had a half-foot cobra in his pants. Apparently the guy was pretty well endowed because they asked him, "What is this snake doing in your pants?" and he replied, "Dating." –BILL MAHER

I just moved in with my boyfriend after having a two-year long-distance relationship. It's nice to do things together for a change. It's nice to go to the movies, have dinner together. Frankly, it's nice to have sex without having MCI involved. –SUE KOLINSKY

If God didn't want you to have sex, he would have changed his name so you wouldn't be able to scream it out when you came. –LOU EISEN

On hockey sounding like an orgy: Gretsky's getting rubbed on the boards, but he just can't seem to get his shot off. –JAY SANKEY

When I was 17 years old, I was going out with a 59-year-old man. Sexually we got along great 'cause the things he couldn't do anymore were the things I didn't know about.

—CAROL HENRY

I'm not embarrassed about having phone sex. You know what's embarrassing about phone sex is that the neighbors can hear me having sex but they don't see anyone enter or leave my apartment. –SUE KOLINSKY

My schoolmates would make love to anything that moved, but I never saw any reason to limit myself. –EMO PHILIPS

A terrible thing happened again last night—nothing. –PHYLLIS DILLER

Enjoy yourself. If you can't enjoy yourself, enjoy somebody else. –JACK SCHAEFER

The walls of my apartment are so thin that when my neighbors have sex, I have an orgasm. –LINDA HERSKOVIC

On condom packaging: They should make them funny. People like to laugh. They should say, "Baby on Board." Put that annoying sign where it belongs once and for all. –ELAYNE BOOSLER

If sex is such a natural phenomenon, how come there are so many books on how to? –BETTE MIDLER

It's strange to think: If you commit sodomy in Georgia, they are going to put you in a cell with another man who's gonna sodomize you. –ROBIN WILLIAMS

Menage-à-trois is a French term. It means "Kodak moment." –GREG RAY

The only thing my mother told me about sex was that I was never going to get any. –DOUG GRAHAM

I practice safe sex. I use an airbag. It's a little startling at first when it flies out. Then the woman realizes it's safer than being thrown clear. –GARRY SHANDLING

They've got a new birth control pill for men now. I think that's fair. It makes a lot more sense to take the bullets out of the gun than to wear a bulletproof vest. –GREG TRAVIS

How is this for a movie scenario: Say that Lorena cuts it off. She then drives to one of those toxic waste dumps and throws it in. Because of the radioactivity and chemicals, it starts to grow way beyond its original size, it grows to about 50 feet and leaves the dump. The Air Force, in response, starts to track its movements. Helicopters are circling over-head. Over the radio, the radio operator asks, "Where's it headed, Bob?" "It looks like it's going in and out of the Holland Tunnel." –ROBIN WILLIAMS

I was 28 when I got married. My husband bought the horse-back riding story. –JOAN RIVERS

I want to die like my father. He died in the sack with a girl 18. He was 57. I guess he came and went at the same time. –RICHARD PRYOR

I got sexually desperate, so I called one of those live sex numbers. I got a girl that stuttered. It cost me 1,500 bucks. –JOHNNY RIZZO

Playboy never wants you to think the pictures are posed. We just happened to catch Kathy typing nude on top of a Volvo this morning in a field. –ELAYNE BOOSLER

It gives me great pleasure to introduce this next comedian. But before I give myself great pleasure… –BUZZ BELMONDO

> # I don't understand S&M. Why go out and beat the crap out of someone who never did anything to you when you can stay home and beat the crap out of someone who did.
>
> —LINDA HERSKOVIC

On the contraceptive sponge: What a great idea. You can have sex and dishes at the same time. Of course, the guy is going, "Honey, I can see myself." –CAROLE MONTGOMERY

On the Lorena Bobbitt incident: I used to think it was safe to use a condom. Now I'm going to use the club. –GARRY SHANDLING

On the Lorena Bobbitt incident: I took out a little sharpy pen. I put a little dotted line around it so my wife would know where to cut and paste. –BOB SAGET

I don't remember having a sexual peak when I was 19—I just remember apologizing a lot. –JEFF STILSON

On phone sex: I saw a phone sex line, 970-PEEE. It's for people who want other people to urinate on them during sex. It's $1.50 for the first minute, 95 cents for each additional minute. Who can pee longer than a minute? Wouldn't you get suspicious after half an hour? "Are you guys running the faucets?" –JON STEWART

And my sex life is nothing to crow about. At my age I'm envious of a stiff wind. –RODNEY DANGERFIELD

I went to a shrink. She hates my guts. She says I have delusions of sexual superiority—she just wants to f - - k me. –JEREMY HOTZ

It's very awkward being a single guy with all the diseases around. You know it's to the point where I won't go to bed with a woman unless she says, "All right, I'll go to bed with you." –GARRY SHANDLING

I'm not into that one-night thing. I think a person should get to know someone and even be in love with them before you use and degrade them. –STEVE MARTIN

It was reported that sex is good for people who suffer from arthritis—it's just not that pleasant to watch. –JAY LENO

I want to show you my breasts and yet I'm frightened. I don't know what it is. But I will touch them. They're fabulous. I had no idea. I think I'll go home with myself. Bye, gotta run. It's so great to be coy with your own body. "Hey, wanna go out?" "Get lost, scum. Beat it." Try spending the night alone with yourself sometime. You wake up the next morning, nobody will ever know what you were doing, not even you. "You wore me out. It was insane. I loved it." –SANDRA BERNHARD

> ## I don't even understand how group sex works. What do they say afterwards? "Excuse me? Was it good for anybody?"
>
> –RITA RUDNER

I did see one new great brand: extra-super sensitive condoms. I thought, "Wow! These must hang around and talk to you after the guy leaves!" –ELAYNE BOOSLER

On dating: I can't even talk to people. I'm so paranoid. I'm afraid they might spit in my eye and kill me. I'm on a date the other night, the girl is talking. I'm just blinking and moving through the whole date. She's like, "What's wrong?" "Stop talking so much, I don't know you that well." I wear contact lenses for protection. –MARIO JOYNER

On edible underwear: I don't know what the big deal is about these. You wear them for a couple of days, they taste just like the other ones. –TOM ARNOLD

On sex with his wife: My wife is a very fortunate person 'cause if I'm videotaping and she falls out of bed funny, she could win $10,000. –BOB SAGET

I was on stage last night talking. I said, "You know the diaphragm is a pain in the ass." Someone yelled out, "You are putting it in the wrong way." –CAROLE MONTGOMERY

On her legs: Peanut butter legs. Brown, smooth, and easy to spread. –LaWanda Page

When I was growing up, we had a petting zoo, and, well, we had two sections. We had a petting zoo and then we had a heavy petting zoo. People who really liked the animals a lot. It was just right over there. It was just more expensive. –Ellen DeGeneres

I was very sheltered growing up. I knew nothing about sex. My mother said this: "Sex is a dirty, disgusting thing you save for somebody you love." –Carol Henry

We keep fighting about sex and money. I mean, she charges me so much, you know. –Rodney Dangerfield

Scientists say that you can get cancer from the radiation thrown off by your electric blanket. I'm so depressed. Here I am, 56 years old, and the most dangerous thing I've ever done in bed is turn on the blanket. –Anita Milner

Sigmund Freud and Carl Jung broke up over the concept of penis envy. Freud thought that every woman wanted a penis. Jung thought that every woman wanted his penis. –Ellen Orchid

What do people mean when they say, "The computer went down on me"? –Marilyn Pittman

How can you have sex without emotional attachment? Use an attachment. –Carrie Snow

[Men] keep rushing through lovemaking. Which is the part I like, the beginning part. Most women are like that. We need time to warm up. Why is this hard for you guys to understand? You are the first people to tell us not to gun a cold engine. You want us to go from zero to sixty in a minute. We're not built like that. We stall. –ANITA WISE

I once made love for an hour and five minutes. It was on the day you push the clocks ahead. –GARRY SHANDLING

After a night out: What did I say? Who did I make out with? Why do these muscles hurt? –JANEANE GAROFALO

Women say it's not how much men have, but what we do with it. How many things can we do with it? What is it, a Cuisinart? It's got two speeds: forward and reverse. –RICHARD JENI

If you can make a woman sing the theme to *Star Trek*, you are doing your job. –SHANG FORBES

The first time we ever made love I said, "Am I the first man that ever made love to you?" She said, "You could be. You look damn familiar." –RONNIE BULLARD

There've been times when I've actually had sex indoors, and then you sober up just a little. When it's over I become like the bartender at 2:00 A.M.: "Okay, people, let's move it out! You don't have to go home, but you can't stay here. Out! Out!" –JANEANE GAROFALO

The only time you ever see a penis in the movies is if a pervert sits down next to you. –ELAYNE BOOSLER

How do you keep the sex fresh? Put it in Tupperware. –GARRY SHANDLING

I said to my husband, "Why don't you call out my name when we are making love?" He said, "I don't want to wake you up." –JOAN RIVERS

Sex is one of the most beautiful, wholesome, and natural things that money can buy. –STEVE MARTIN

Every time we make love, my boyfriend keeps telling me to tell him when I'm having an orgasm—which is difficult, 'cause usually when I'm having one, he's not there.
–MARGO BLACK

Every woman must learn to fake orgasm. It's common courtesy.

–JOAN RIVERS

Have you heard of this new book entitled *1,001 Sex Secrets Men Should Know*? It contains comments from 1,001 different women on how men can be better in bed. I think that women would actually settle for three: Slow down, turn off the TV, call out the right name. –JAY LENO

My uncle got a vasectomy. Put it on MasterCard. Forgot to pay. The finance company came over and knocked up his wife. –ELAYNE BOOSLER

A survey asking men who they would want to be stranded with on a desert island has Pamela Anderson tied with Sharon Stone. Of course, the number one choice was Pamela Anderson tied to Sharon Stone. –CONAN O'BRIEN

On her ex-husband Tom Arnold: In lovemaking, what he lacked in size, he made up for in speed. –ROSEANNE

Why is Wednesday called "hump day" when most people get laid on the weekends? –JEFF MARDER

Everybody has sex now. When I was a kid, only women had sex. You had to get it from them. –TONY STONE

Nice guys finish last. What's wrong with that? Isn't that what most women want? –BOB ETTINGER

On oral sex: When are some men going to realize that it's a treat, not a duty?...You know what I hate: guys that bring rubber bands to tie back your hair. I don't make this stuff up. I just write it down when I see it. Trust me. When a man shows up on a date with a lot of rubber bands on his wrist, he is not the paperboy. –DIANE NICHOLS

Men will say, "I'll call you. I'll call you." When they say they're going to call, they don't, and when they say they're not gonna come, they do. –CAROL HENRY

On condoms: There's probably not a person in America who can look good taking one of these off. –ELAYNE BOOSLER

Low self-esteem sex is bad. This is sad. When I have an orgasm, I shriek, "I'm sorry." –RICHARD LEWIS

At Your Own Risk

Poor Lou Gehrig. Died of Lou Gehrig's Disease. How the hell do you not see that comin', you know?
–DENIS LEARY

When you go to prison they take away your shoelaces so you can't kill yourself. I wouldn't know how to kill myself with shoelaces. You'd have to be the McGyver of killing yourself.

—MARK FARRELL

We live in a country where John Lennon takes six bullets in the chest—Yoko Ono is standing right next to him—not one f - - kin' bullet! Explain that to me! –DENIS LEARY

To me, an elevator is a coffin on a string. Dangling over an abyss. It's like a casket yo-yo. Remember the plane crash in the Andes? When the survivors ate the dead passengers? I'm not proud of this but when I take an elevator, I bring a knife and fork and pray for fat passengers. –CAROLYN MAY

I wonder how you can lose your dick and not know it. When do you suddenly wake up a Ken Doll? Does she get on the phone with a friend and say, "He abuses me all the time"? The friend tells her, "Then throw the prick out." –ROBIN WILLIAMS

Jack and Jill went up the hill both with a buck and a quarter. Jill came down with two-fifty. Oh, that f - - king whore. –ANDREW DICE CLAY

Art Fleming, the original host of the TV show *Jeopardy!* , passed away recently. Sadly, doctors ignored his request for help because it was not in the form of a question. –BILL MAHER

That Jeffrey Dahmer character. The guy ate 17 people. I understand one or two. But 17, you are eating just to eat.... They found those heads rotting in the refrigerator. That shouldn't happen. Those go in the crisper.... They found a jar of testicles. A jar of testicles! It's like "Hey, what did you eat for breakfast? Nut in honey?" –BRUCE BAUM

I think assisting suicide should be legal. Especially if the person you're assisting has a rent-controlled apartment. Why should I suffer any longer? –JANINE DITULLIO

Little Boy Blue, he needed the money. –ANDREW DICE CLAY

Why do dead people get to ride in such nice cars? That can piss you off if you're on the bus. –MARSHA WARFIELD

What was the name of the little boy whose nuts grew every time he told a lie? Pistachio. –TOMMY SLEDGE

I would never do crack. I would never do a drug named after a part of my own ass, okay, folks? –DENIS LEARY

I'm the kind of guy who tells an angry albino to lighten up. –SHANG FORBES

Tragedy is when I cut my finger. Comedy is when you fall into an open sewer and die. –MEL BROOKS

In Los Angeles, McDonald's quickly reacted to the highway shootings. They came out with "Happy To Be Alive Meals." –AL CLETHEN

I had so much electricity running through me I could read by my testicles. –ROBIN WILLIAMS

On Maxipads with wings: I'd be afraid to buy these things. You go walking into a supermarket and try to be inconspicuous. "Excuse me, sir. Where are the Maxipads?" "Ah, hell they could be anywhere today. Don't ask me. They got wings, they got the run of the store. I put a box down over there at six o'clock. They could be in frozen foods by now. I pack 'em. You track 'em." –MARIO JOYNER

And you know what Hell is, folks? It's Andy Gibb singing "Shadow Dancing" for eons and eons. –DENIS LEARY

New York really messes up your perspective, doesn't it? Even in the little things. Like the other night I was watching *The Diary of Anne Frank*. Now I used to have a normal reaction to that movie—I felt bad for that poor family trapped in their tiny little attic. Now I'm looking at it going, "This is a great apartment. That skylight, that bookcase you go through—it's fabulous." –FRANK MAYA

Three blind mice. See how they run. Where the f - - k are they going? –ANDREW DICE CLAY

They always have signs in restaurant bathrooms: "Employees wash hands before leaving restrooms." Apparently, patrons can pee all over themselves and paw freely at the salad bar. Shouldn't everybody have to wash up? "Hey, Bob, you've tinkled all over yourself." "I don't work here, screw 'em." –JACKIE BLYNN

That was the only good thing about the 1980s—we got rid of one of the Bee Gees. One down, three to go, that's what I say, folks. –DENIS LEARY

If I lived in Anne Frank's place, I'm sure I would have written *No Exit*. –BETSY SALKIND

I'm over at Elvis's house, banging on the bathroom door, yelling, "Hey, Elvis, I gotta go. What did you do, die in there?" –CAPTAIN ROWDY

Yeah man, let's not talk about mothers, man. Let's get off of mothers. I just got off yours. –DAMON WAYANS

I couldn't go home for Passover this year because I had a yeast infection. –BETSY SALKIND

> I was listening to a Hendrix CD the other day and I thought, "Hey, man, those CDs are so clean, you can hear the needle going in his arm."
>
> –SHANG FORBES

How did Captain Hook die? He wiped with the wrong hand. –TOMMY SLEDGE

Foul Shots

I think sports stars make great role models, particularly if you are thinking about a career in crime.

–LAURA KIGHTLINGER

Yankee pitcher Jack McDowell gave the finger to the crowd. He was fined $5,000 and given a New York City cab license. –Conan O'Brien

The only sport we could watch was bowling. One big black ball rolling into the ten white pins. All with red necks. –Warren Hutcherson

Although golf was originally restricted to wealthy, overweight Protestants, today it's open to anybody who owns hideous clothing. – Dave Barry

Tennis is like marrying for money. Love has nothing to do with it.

–Phyllis Diller

I worry about the germs in the holes of bowling balls. Nobody cleans those holes. There are years of impacted pizza fingers in there. Taco fingers. Chicken fingers. I'm amazed those balls still have holes. Ever smell a bowling ball hole? You think the balls are knocking down the pins? You're wrong. The pins are passing out from the smell. –Carolyn May

Football is a fair sport for my people. It's the only sport in the world where a Negro can chase a white man and 40,000 people stand up to cheer him. –Dick Gregory

I'm not overweight—it's Steve Garvey's love baby. –Bobcat Goldthwait

I went fishing with a dotted line and caught every other fish. –Steven Wright

I went hunting for the first time. I shot an elk. I felt bad at first, but the guy was wearing a plaid leisure suit so he pretty much had it coming. –BRIAN KILEY

I like sports. But I'm over 30 so I don't have to be good at sports anymore. When I was 15 or 16 years old I would dive for the ball. Now when I play softball, if the ball is more than five feet away on either side of me, I say, "It's a home run!" I'm not spillin' my beer for anything. –JOHN MENDOZA

I play on New York City's only women's hockey team. It's nice when my teammates come see me perform. We so rarely get to see one another's shoes. –LYNN HARRIS

One of the players is a therapist. She scored a goal the last game and I had the "assist." After the game, she thanked me for enabling her. –LYNN HARRIS

We do play rough. We have checking. The only difference between men's and women's hockey is women check, but then they apologize. –LYNN HARRIS

I love boxing. Where else do two grown men prance around in satin underwear, fighting over a belt?…The one who wins gets a purse. They do it in gloves. It's the accessory connection I love. –JOHN MCGIVERN

The reason most people play golf is to wear clothes they would not be caught dead in otherwise. –ROGER SIMON

What amazes me is the credits that run at the end of the fishing show. There are two guys fishing and 90 people involved. –BRIAN REGAN

Cross-country skiing is great if you live in a small country. –STEVEN WRIGHT

Police have arrested the man who was pictured throwing snowballs at Giants Stadium. If convicted, he [may] face six months in jail and a $1,000 fine. If it turns out he was under the influence of alcohol or drugs, he'll be signed by the Yankees. –DAVID LETTERMAN

What a life. When I was a kid I asked my dad if I could go ice skating. He told me to wait until it gets warmer. –RODNEY DANGERFIELD

On entertaining during the Super Bowl: I'm making 50 pigs in a blanket for 20 pigs in the living room. –ROSEANNE

I don't believe for a second weightlifting is a sport. They pick up a heavy thing and put it down again. To me, that's indecision. –PAULA POUNDSTONE

I used to go fishing until it struck me: You can buy fish. What the hell am I doing in a boat at four-thirty in the morning? If I want a hamburger, I don't track cattle down. –KENNY POTCHENSON

Women always cheer in full sentences like, "You have the right idea!" "Share with your neighbor." "The wings need to be on the boards—ideally." "You totally don't look fat!" –LYNN HARRIS

I'm into golf now. I'm getting pretty good. I can almost hit the ball as far as I can throw the clubs.

–BOB ETTINGER

I see a lot of bicycles with baby seats on the back. Is this really fun for the kid? Dad's enjoying the fresh air and sunshine. Junior's got his nose wedged between sweaty butt cheeks all afternoon. –JONATHAN DROLL

Seventy-five percent of your body heat is lost through the top of your head. Which sounds like you could go skiing naked if you got a good hat. –JERRY SEINFELD

I watched a fishing show today on TV. Have you ever watched fishing for about 15 minutes and said, "Boy, I need a life"? –BRIAN REGAN

> **Because of the pressure that Attorney General Janet Reno has been putting on the networks to cut down on the violence on TV, CBS has announced that they are dropping figure skating.**
>
> –DAVID LETTERMAN

My biggest fear is that Tonya Harding will quit skating and take up stand up. –GARRY SHANDLING

You might be a redneck if you've been too drunk to fish. –JEFF FOXWORTHY

I'm glad men don't get pregnant. Football season would be ruined— "Montana is knocked up again." –JEFF STILSON

The poor film editor for the fishing shows. This guy has to watch all the footage that just wasn't exciting enough to make it into the final product. –BRIAN REGAN

Wherever You Go, There You Are

*There are eight
million stories in the naked city
—and most of them shouldn't be heard.*
–BETTE MIDLER

The Places You'll Go—
The People You'll Meet

Fall is my favorite season in L.A., watching the birds change color and fall from the trees. –DAVID LETTERMAN

There are parts of Texas now where Jack-in-the-Box restaurants are accepting the Mexican currency as payment. What is worse is that they have lowered the drive-in window so that you can hand the food directly into the trunk. –BILL MAHER

I don't have a problem with San Francisco parking. I drive a forklift. –JIM SAMUELS

I think I know how Chicago got started. A bunch of people in New York said, "Gee, I'm enjoying the crime and the poverty, but it just isn't cold enough. Let's go West."
–RICHARD JENI

Boston is, in fact, the drinkingest town I've ever been in my entire life. I've never seen a town drunk more as an aggregate. Do you ever just wake up as a city collectively and go, "Hey, what did we do last night?" –JON STEWART

New York now leads the world's great cities in the number of people around whom you shouldn't make a sudden move.
–DAVID LETTERMAN

I grew up in the Bronx. It was no picnic growing up in the Bronx. In the Bronx, there was no grass. –LINDA HERSKOVIC

It's nice to be here in Tempe where a baby's first words are, "But it's dry heat." –DENNIS MILLER

I was born in Alabama. I only lived there for a month until I did everything there was to do. –PAULA POUNDSTONE

The Swiss have an interesting army. Five hundred years without a war. Pretty impressive. Also pretty lucky for them. Ever see that little Swiss Army knife they have to fight with? Not much of a weapon there. Corkscrews. Bottle openers. "Come on buddy, let's go. You get past me, the guy in back of me, he's got a spoon. Back off. I've got the toe clippers right here." –JERRY SEINFELD

Everything is drive-through. In California they even have a burial service called Jump-in-the-Box. –WIL SHRINER

Traffic signals in New York are just rough guidelines.
–DAVID LETTERMAN

A couple of weeks ago I was in New York City.... It rained while I was there. That wasn't all that bad because in the rain, New York City makes its own gravy. –JAKE JOHANSEN

Miami? It's a place where 1000 different nationalities get together and give each other the finger on I-95.
–RICHARD JENI

A two-pound turkey and a 50-pound cranberry—that's Thanksgiving dinner at Three Mile Island.

–JOHNNY CARSON

I work at the local radio station in New York. What I do is get in my car during rush hour and report on helicopter traffic. –JOE BOLSTER

> I am originally from the Ozarks. Not everyone in the Ozarks lives in a trailer park. There's a huge waiting list.
>
> —NANCY NORTON

One important thing came out of the Persian Gulf War. They now have a Playboy Channel in Kuwait where the women do naughty things—like work and vote. –DENISE MUNRO

In New York City, it has gotten hot and humid. Your strength is gone. For the last two weeks, New Yorkers have been giving each other only half a finger. –DAVID LETTERMAN

My father is the mayor of the town right now. It's a small town so eventually everyone gets to be the mayor. He is the mayor right now. They elected the mayor by radio last year. My dad was the fifth caller....We're proud of him. He is a quick dialer. –JAKE JOHANSEN

I was at a bookstore here on Melrose and I asked a clerk if they had any books written by the Brontë sisters, and she said, "I didn't know those little girls on *Full House* could spell." –BRETT BUTLER

You get off in Israel, "Welcome to Israel. The Holy Land." "Great, I'm from America. Home of the Whopper. Nice to see you." –JON STEWART

I'm from Georgia originally. I live in California now. Out there, people always make fun of the way I talk. I keep telling them you're gonna be real surprised when you get to heaven and St. Peter says, "Y'all get in the truck. We're going up to the big house." –JEFF FOXWORTHY

It was tragic. They arrested an Amish man and put him in jail. Think about it. It's terrible. It's worse than me and you. Take him down there. Give him that one phone call. Who the hell is he going to call? None of his friends have telephones. –MARIO JOYNER

People in New York are always in a hurry. When you call 911 the operator says, "This better be good." –DAVID LETTERMAN

Have you ever wondered what makes Californians so calm? Besides drugs, I mean. The answer is hot tubs. A hot tub is a redwood container filled with water that you sit in naked with members of the opposite sex, none of whom is necessarily your spouse. After a few hours in their hot tubs, Californians don't give a damn about earthquakes or mass murderers. They don't give a damn about anything, which is why they were able to produce *Laverne and Shirley* week after week. –DAVE BARRY

I took some jobs for the exposure and publicity. The next thing I know I got a job down in a small town in Alabama...so small they are still excited about the wheel. –MARGARET SMITH

Things are just too sophisticated out there in L.A. If guys fall in love, they think they have to buy wine and candy and roses. Hell, in the South, when we fall in love, we just spray-paint your name on an overpass. –JEFF FOXWORTHY

On going home: I don't get to Iowa very often. It took me a long time to realize that we were free to go. –JAKE JOHANSEN

There are weird names for towns in the South. I drove through a town named Lynchburg. I went through that town 90 miles an hour. –MARIO JOYNER

So I go to some pretty rural places talking about being gay and I'm Jewish as well so I'm just this big hatred double coupon. –SCOTT SILVERMAN

In California, we have a different kind of police. You get stopped in West Hollywood, "Stop! Those shoes don't go with those pants." –ROBIN WILLIAMS

I'm from Downers Grove, Illinois. We had a blackout there the other day, but fortunately the police made him get back into his car before he got too far. –EMO PHILIPS

Another ad in the paper said, "We guarantee our furniture. We stand behind it for 6 months...." That's the reason I left the Soviet Union. –YAKOV SMIRNOFF

I met a man from Chernobyl, a technician. I asked him if the problem was that severe. He said, "Whoof, whoof...meow." –BILLY CRYSTAL

In England, if you commit a crime, the police don't have a gun and you don't have a gun. If you commit a crime, "Stop, or I'll say stop again." –ROBIN WILLIAMS

I wanted to get out of Russia. It's not easy to get out. You apply for a visa. They give you MasterCard. There is nothing like American Express. There's Russian Express: Don't Leave Home. –YAKOV SMIRNOFF

If they opened a Taco Bell in Mexico, what would the slogan be? "Stay where you are"? –GEORGE LOPEZ

On a reunited Germany: If there is a man amongst us who sees why these two should not be joined together, let him speak now or forever hold his piece...in the ready position with the safety off. –DENNIS MILLER

Being a New Yorker is never having to say you are sorry.
–LILY TOMLIN

"I'm going to be a big star!" In California, we call that sort of statement creative visualization. In the other 49 states, it's called self-delusion. –MAUREEN BROWNSEY

Motto for New Jersey: "What died?" – STEVEN PEARL

Motto for New York: "What the hell are you looking at?"
–STEVEN PEARL

A lot of people up North, they think everybody from the South is married to their sister and has seen a UFO. I told them, "I'm just dating my sister and couldn't swear that it wasn't a weather balloon." –JEFF FOXWORTHY

Be glad you live on this side of the cultural warp. There are guys in West Virginia building additions on mobile homes. It's the kind of place where they test-market Dynasty cologne. –DENNIS MILLER

I'm Canadian—it's like American, but without a gun.

–THE KIDS IN THE HALL

Up until a month ago, people in New York were being killed for their coats. I don't think that's right. If you are gonna kill someone for their coat, I think you should eat them too.
–LAURA KIGHTLINGER

I joined a health club. In L.A., you have to do that to get your driver's license. –RICHARD JENI

The big exciting news from Birmingham and all around the state of Alabama is the new Mercedes plant. All I got to say is I hope the things are easy to put together. –MICKEY DEAN

We're an interracial couple, my wife and I. I'm from Kentucky and she's not a relative. –MARK KLEIN

We live in a mobile home. Hey, there are advantages to living in a mobile home. One time, it caught on fire. We met the fire department halfway there. –RONNIE SHAKES

Oklahoma City is probably the only city in the country where you pull a Ford Fairmont into the parking lot and people come out to admire your car. –BRUCE BAUM

I just got back from England. Had a hard time fitting in. So I tried to make myself feel comfortable, hang out in the black community. But both of those brothers were having a hard time fitting in too. –DAVE CHAPPELLE

The United States is like the guy at the party who gives cocaine to everybody and still nobody likes him. –JIM SAMUELS

I like Florida. I went to high school down there in Clearwater. Clearwater High School. We were the Clearwater Tornadoes. The only other team we ever beat was the Palm Harbor Mobile Homes. –DAVID KINNEY

In Oregon, they bungee jump from balloons. Doesn't that mean that at some crucial point, there's a very important transition from jumper to anchor? –JOHN RODGERS

Things are bad all over. I was in Beverly Hills and people were standing on croissant lines. And when you're in Beverly Hills, you've got to go to the Tomb of the Unknown Servant. –STEVE BLUESTEIN

In New York when someone puts a knife to your chest you give them your money. In L.A. when someone puts a knife to your chest, you give them your money, you say "Thank you doctor," and buy a bigger bra. –DEIDRE SULLIVAN

In North America, the United States is the exciting one and Canada is the boring sensible one. It's like we're the designated driver of North America. –JOHN RODGERS

I have low self-esteem, it comes from my childhood. I was born in Lancaster County, Pennsylvania. It wasn't easy. You don't know what it's like to grow up in an Amish family when you are into drugs and you're a sex addict. What do you do? Churn butter naked? Masturbate with a pretzel rod? –JOAN KEITER

Where can an Italian get Jewish food cooked by a Mexican in an Asian deli? Only in New York.

–TIM HALPERN

French people think they are so sexy. Sitting in these cafes chain smoking. "I had un cappuccino. Un croissant. Who wants my diseases? Anyone want my diseases?" –PAULY SHORE

Why are there interstate highways in Hawaii? –THE ATOMIC CAFE

On living in New York: I'm oblivious to everything. I just don't notice things anymore. I sat in a coffee shop, drank

half a cup of coffee before I noticed there was lipstick on the cup. There was wadded-up gum and lipstick on the napkin. I must have been sitting on that woman's lap for an hour.
–LAURA KIGHTLINGER

I was just down in Memphis. Went to Graceland. Go if you've never been. Nothing like being ripped off by a dead hillbilly. –DREW CAREY

Anytime four New Yorkers get into a cab together without arguing, a bank robbery has just taken place. –JOHNNY CARSON

I was born in Alabama and raised in Georgia. I'm so Southern I'm related to myself. I'm the type of Southern Baptist that keeps a picture of Elvis's Last Supper in our living room.... Whenever I mention that in my nightclub act, I usually get at least one irate Baptist who says, "You can make fun of Jesus, but leave the King out of it."

–BRETT BUTLER

Getting There Is Half the Fun

On driving from L.A. to New York: You have to pass through that middle area of the country. Miles and miles of Oklahoma, Nebraska, and Missouri. The only thing on the radio for hours and hours was Rush Limbaugh. God must have been looking at a map of the United States and gone, "Gay people get to the sides." –GEORGIA RAGSDALE

At the Dallas–Fort Worth Airport, a man was arrested for running naked through the airport. It turns out that he was with the mile-high club and he was trying to make a connecting flight. –JAY LENO

I went to the airport. I had three pieces of luggage. I said that I want this piece to go to Cleveland, this piece to Toronto, and this piece to Florida. The airline agent said, "We can't do that." I replied, "Well, you did it last week." –HENNY YOUNGMAN

I think I embarrassed the lady next to me on the plane. I was on one of those flights that you sleep on…and I sleep in the nude. –JOHNNY DARK

My wife and I went to Spain for our honeymoon. We get to fly for free because of my wife's job. She's a terrorist. –BRIAN KILEY

My license plate says PMS. Nobody cuts me off. –WENDY LIEBMAN

I think all cars should have car phones in them and the license plate should be the phone number. You could call them up and tell them to get the hell out of the way. Old people would have the 1-800 numbers. 1-800-MOVE-IT-MURRAY. –JOHN MENDOZA

On driving: Ugly thoughts come up....There've been times when I'm stuck on the freeway and I think to myself, "If half the city died right now, I'd be home already." –PAUL REISER

Have you noticed? Anyone going slower than you is an idiot, and anyone going faster than you is a moron. –GEORGE CARLIN

I had to stop driving my car for a while...the tires got dizzy. –STEVEN WRIGHT

I remember learning to drive on my dad's lap. Did you guys ever do that? He'd work the brakes. I'd work the wheel. Then I went to take the driver's test and sat on the examiner. I failed the exam. But he still writes to me. That's the really nice part. –GARRY SHANDLING

The best car safety device is a rear-view mirror with a cop in it. –DUDLEY MOORE

Why do they call it rush hour when nothing moves?

–ROBIN WILLIAMS

Wild Kingdom

> *Why does*
> *Sea World have a seafood restaurant?*
> *I'm halfway through my fishburger*
> *and I realize, "Oh my God*
> *—I could be eating a slow learner!"*
> –LYNDA MONTGOMERY

Chihuahua. There's a waste of dog food. Chihuahua looks like a dog that is still far away. –BILLIAM CORONEL

I will not eat oysters. I want my food dead. Not sick, wounded, and dead. –WOODY ALLEN

We're having something a little different this year for Thanksgiving. Instead of a turkey, we're having a swan. You get more stuffing. –GEORGE CARLIN

I'm not a vegetarian because I love animals. I am a vegetarian because I hate plants.

–A. WHITNEY BROWN

I like dogs. I do. But they're not that bright, really. Let's examine the dog mind: Every time you come home, he thinks it's amazing. He can't believe that you've accomplished this again. You walk in the door. The joy of it almost kills him. "He's back again! It's that guy! It's that guy!" –JERRY SEINFELD

Stuffed deer heads on walls are bad enough, but it's worse when they are wearing dark glasses and have streamers and ornaments in their antlers because then you know they were enjoying themselves at a party when they were shot. –ELLEN DEGENERES

I bought a bird feeder. It was expensive, but I figured in the long run, it would save me money on cat food. –LINDA HERSKOVIC

Did you ever walk into a room and forget why you walked in? I think that's how dogs spend their lives. –SUE MURPHY

I don't kill flies, but I like to mess with their minds. I hold them above globes. They freak out and yell, "Whooa, I'm way too high!" –BRUCE BAUM

I was at a friend's house and his dog took a dump on the rug. My friend turned to the dog and said, "Did you do that?" I felt bad for the dog. So I said, "No, I did it." So he hit me with a newspaper. –JOHN MENDOZA

My parakeet died. We were playing badminton. –DANNY CURTIS

On going to a farm with the farmer: He played a practical joke on me. He let me milk his bull. I learned something: You milk this animal once, you have a friend for life. –YAKOV SMIRNOFF

Dogs come when they're called. Cats take a message and get back to you. –MISSY DIZICK

I take my pet lion to church every Sunday. He has to eat. –MARTY POLLIO

Bring me a live cow over to the table. I'll carve off what I want and ride the rest home. –DENIS LEARY

On Sea World's killer whales: For $35 [admission] they should be chewing on people's skulls and spitting them into the audience, not jumping up and kissing people. –SEAN TWEEDLEY

I had a cockroach infestation. At first, I started killing them, but then I felt guilty because I'm a member of PETA. So I thought it would be better if they just killed each other. So I've introduced drugs into their community. It's not working out very well. Things have escalated. I have to start a war on drugs. That's not working out either because they are paying off the cats. –BETSY SALKIND

Do you think animals have groupies? Do you think there is a French poodle hanging around outside saying, "I f - - ked seven Lassies. Morris the Cat? I f - - ked him too." –ROBIN WILLIAMS

I try to get my dog to practice safe sex. But he keeps licking the condoms off.

–TIM HALPERN

Why does McDonald's have to count every burger that they sell? What is their ultimate goal? Do they want cows surrendering voluntarily? They should just put on their signs, "McDonald's—We're doing very well." –JERRY SEINFELD

I had a linguistics professor who said that it's man's ability to use language that makes him the dominant species on the planet. That may be. But I think there's one other thing that separates us from animals: We aren't afraid of vacuum cleaners. –JEFF STILSON

I like Yorkshire terriers. They're good to wash your car with. They fit right in the bucket, which is good. Hold your breath. "Swoosh." Then you go get a blow dryer, put a stick up their butts and dust the furniture. –BILLIAM CORONEL

Did you ever notice when you blow in a dog's face he gets mad at you? But when you take him in a car he sticks his head out the window. –STEVE BLUESTONE

I ask people why they have deer heads on their walls. They always say, "Because it's such a beautiful animal." There you go! I think my mother is attractive, but I have photographs of her. –ELLEN DEGENERES

You know why dogs have no money? No pockets. 'Cause they see change on the street all the time and it's driving them crazy. When you're walking them. He is always looking up at you. "There's a quarter…" –JERRY SEINFELD

Do you think that birds that live at airports have a bad self-image? –DENNIS MILLER

My dog watches me on TV. So, if I may take this opportunity, "No! No! No!" –GARRY SHANDLING

> ## I had a great Earth Day. I drove around with my muffler off, flicking butts out the window. Then I hit a deer. It's okay. I never hit a deer unless I intend to eat it.
>
> –DREW CAREY

"Thou shall not kill. Thou shall not commit adultery. Don't eat pork." I'm sorry, what was that last one? "Don't eat pork." God has spoken. Is that the word of God or is that pigs trying to outsmart everybody? –JON STEWART

You Know
You're Ugly
When...

*You know, a lot of girls
go out with me to further their
careers.... Damn anthropologists.*
–EMO PHILIPS

I was a poster child...for birth control! –RODNEY DANGERFIELD

At the end of your life if you can count all your friends you have, your really good friends, on one hand...you know you've been spending a lot of time alone in your room. –BOB SAGET

I could have been your father but the dog beat me over the fence. –DARRELL HAMMOND

You mother is so fat that when she get on the scale, it says, "To be continued." –DAMON WAYANS

Some women hold up dresses that are so ugly and they always say the same thing. "This looks much better on." On what? On fire? –RITA RUDNER

I joined gamblers anonymous—they gave me two to one I wouldn't make it! –RODNEY DANGERFIELD

You are looking at the ugliest kid ever born in Larchmont, New York. The doctor looked at me and said, "She's not done yet," and shoved me back in.

–JOAN RIVERS

I'm driving her home all right, and that's when I start to wonder if there's going to be any sex—and if I'm gonna be involved. –GARRY SHANDLING

I put on a peek-a-boo blouse. He peeked, and booed. –PHYLLIS DILLER

We have friends who have the ugliest child you've ever seen. They walked out of the pet store with this child and the alarm went off. –JEFF FOXWORTHY

When I was born, my mother looked at me and looked at the afterbirth and screamed, "Twins!" –JOAN RIVERS

I remember the advice that my old man gave me. He told me never take candy from a stranger unless he offered me a ride. –RODNEY DANGERFIELD

You mother is so fat she's gotta take her pants off just to get in her pockets. –DAMON WAYANS

I was so ugly they sent my picture to *Ripley's Believe It or Not.* They sent it back, "I don't believe it." –JOAN RIVERS

When I go the beach, even the tide won't come in. –PHYLLIS DILLER

I have no self-confidence. When girls tell me yes, I tell them to think it over. –RODNEY DANGERFIELD

I discovered my wife in bed with another man, and I was crushed. So I said, "Get off of me, you two." –EMO PHILIPS

Ain't nothing wrong with a weave…if you want some hair. But at least try to fool somebody. If you are baldheaded on Monday, you can't have hair down to your butt on Wednesday. –SINBAD

When I was a kid, I had two friends, and they were imaginary and they would only play with each other. –RITA RUDNER

I have so little sex appeal that my gynecologist calls me sir.
–JOAN RIVERS

> My girlfriend. She's not good looking or anything. I took her to a Country & Western bar and somebody tried to ride her. "Where's the quarter go?" They couldn't figure it out.
>
> –DREW CAREY

You sister is so ugly they gotta tie pork chops on her neck so that the dog will play with her. –DAMON WAYANS

I think my agent hates me. He put me up for a snuff film. It's a three-picture deal. –BETSY SALKIND

Some Final Thoughts...

*Always look out
for number one—and be careful
not to step in number two.*
–RODNEY DANGERFIELD

Reality is a collective hunch. –LILY TOMLIN AND JANE WAGNER

Why are our days numbered and not, say, lettered?
–WOODY ALLEN

Why is there so much pressure to spend Independence Day with other people? –BETSY SALKIND

God is a great humorist. He just has a slow audience to work with. –GARRISON KEILLOR

Oh, friends are just enemies who don't have enough guts to kill you. –JUDY TENUTA

Why is it that when we talk to God we're said to be praying but when God talks to us we're schizophrenic? –LILY TOMLIN

> I stay away from the miserable people, because misery loves company. Just look at a fly strip. You never see a fly stuck there saying, "Go around! Go around!"
>
> –MARGARET SMITH

How is it possible to find meaning in a finite world, given my waist and shirt size? –WOODY ALLEN

It's not easy becoming a stand-up comic. It's like becoming a murderer. No matter how much people try to talk you out of it, you are going to do it. –JERRY SEINFELD

Not only is there no God, but try getting a plumber on weekends. –WOODY ALLEN

Nothing is impossible. Some things are just less likely than others. –JONATHAN WINTERS

We're all in this alone. –LILY TOMLIN

My one regret in life is that I'm not someone else.
–WOODY ALLEN

> **A good rule of thumb is if you've made it to 35 and your job still requires you to wear a nametag, you've probably made a serious vocational error.**
>
> –DENNIS MILLER

You know what I hate? Indian givers...no, I take that back.
–EMO PHILIPS

I never know how much of what I say is true. –BETTE MIDLER

Reality is a crutch for people who can't cope with drugs.
–LILY TOMLIN

I don't know the key to success, but the key to failure is to try to please everybody. –BILL COSBY

Say it, don't spray it. –PEE WEE HERMAN

I do not believe in an afterlife, although I am bringing a change of underwear. –WOODY ALLEN

Life is something you do when you can't get to sleep.
–FRAN LEBOWITZ

In spite of the cost of living, it's still popular. –KATHY NORRIS

To you I'm an atheist. To God, I'm the Loyal Opposition.
–WOODY ALLEN

It's a rare person who doesn't want to hear what he doesn't want to hear. –DICK CAVETT

Eternal nothingness is fine if you happened to be dressed for it. –WOODY ALLEN

That is the saving grace of humor. If you fail, no one is laughing at you. –A. WHITNEY BROWN

No matter how cynical you get, it is impossible to keep up.
–LILY TOMLIN

If life was fair, Elvis would be alive and all the impersonators would be dead. –JOHNNY CARSON

On the plus side, death is one of the few things that can be done just as easily lying down. –WOODY ALLEN

If you've read a lot of books you are considered well-read, but if you watch a lot of TV, you're not considered well-viewed. –LILY TOMLIN

I know you are, but what am I? –PEE WEE HERMAN

As long as people will accept crap, it will be financially profitable to dispense it. –DICK CAVETT

Reality is the leading cause of stress for those in touch with it. –JANE WAGNER

Whining is anger through a small opening. –STUART SMALLEY

I couldn't wait for success, so I went ahead without it. –JONATHAN WINTERS

If truth is beauty, how come no one has their hair done in the library? –LILY TOMLIN

I know what cheese is and I know what wiz is, so why do I eat Cheez Wiz?

–KERRY TALMAGES

A fool and his money were lucky to get together in the first place. –HARRY ANDERSON

Life is full of misery, loneliness and suffering, and it's all over much too soon. –WOODY ALLEN

Everything that used to be a sin is now a disease. –BILL MAHER

The trouble with the rat race is that even if you win you are still a rat. –LILY TOMLIN

We all enter the world in the same way: naked, screaming, soaked in blood. But if you live your life right, that kind of thing doesn't have to stop right there. –DANA GOULD

The
Green
Room

Meet the Comedians

TIM ALLEN: Star of the film *The Santa Clause* and of ABC's *Home Improvement.* Author of the best-selling *Don't Stand Too Close to a Naked Man.*

WOODY ALLEN: Academy Award–winning director; writer, and actor of several films including *Annie Hall* and *Hannah and Her Sisters.*

STEVE ALTMAN: Appeared on numerous comedy shows including VH-1's *Comedy Spotlight* and A&E's *Caroline's Comedy Hour.*

TOM ARNOLD: Actor who has appeared in the films *True Lies* and *Nine Months.* Former co-star of ABC's *Roseanne.* Starred in the former ABC sitcom *The Jackie Thomas Show.*

MICHAEL ARONIN: Comedian with cerebral palsy who says that in high school he was voted the Most Likely to Get a Parking Space.

KILLER BEAZ: Appeared on A&E's *Comedy on the Road.* Three-time winner of Showtime's Funniest Person in Mississippi contest.

ROB BECKER: Star of the one-man Broadway show, *Defending the Caveman.*

JOY BEHAR: Actress who appeared in Nora Ephron's film *This Is My Life.* Featured "patient" on Comedy Central's *Dr. Katz, Professional Therapist.*

SUZY BERGER: "Out" comedian who has appeared on National Public Radio.

SANDRA BERNHARD: Co-star of ABC's *Roseanne.*

STEVE BLUESTEIN: Segment producer for the former Fox show *Totally Hidden Videos.* Former writer for Norman Lear.

ELAYNE BOOSLER: Actress and writer who has been featured in numerous comedy specials, including her own for HBO.

STEVE BRINDER: Stand-up comedian and teacher.

STEVE BRUNER: Appeared on A&E's *An Evening at the Improv.* Writer for both the Showtime and Fox networks.

RONNIE BULLARD: Appeared on A&E's *Comedy on the Road.*

BRETT BUTLER: Star of ABC's *Grace Under Fire.* Author of *Knee Deep In Paradise.*

DREW CAREY: Star of ABC's *The Drew Carey Show.*

GEORGE CARLIN: Starred in the former Fox sitcom *The George Carlin Show.* Carlin has won a Grammy, was nominated for an Emmy, and won a CableAce award.

JIM CARREY: Star of the films *Dumb and Dumber, The Mask* and two *Ace Ventura* films. Co-star of the former Fox skit-com *In Living Color.*

JOHNNY CARSON: Hosted NBC's *The Tonight Show* for more than 30 years.

CHRISTOPHER CASE: Appeared on Comedy Central's *Stand Up Stand Up*.

DICK CAVETT: Host of CNBC's *The Dick Cavett Show*. Has appeared on Broadway and in plays at the Williamstown Theater Festival. Got his start as a writer for NBC's *The Tonight Show* in 1960.

MARGARET CHO: Starred in the former ABC comedy *All American Girl*.

ANDREW DICE CLAY: Star of the film *Ford Fairlane*. Starred in the former CBS sitcom *Bless This House*.

KATE CLINTON: "Out" comedian and 15-year veteran of the stand-up circuit.

JAFFE COHEN: "Out" comedian and co-author of *Growing Up Gay: From Left Out to Coming Out*.

MICHAEL COLYAR: Appeared on numerous television shows including Comedy Central's *Comic Justice*.

BILLIAM CORONEL: Appeared on A&E's *Caroline's Comedy Hour* and Comedy Central's *The A List*. He wrote and performed on the former Fox Show *Comic Strip Live*.

BILL COSBY: Actor, writer, educator and philanthropist. Starred in the former NBC sitcom *The Cosby Show*. Author of the best-selling *Fatherhood*.

JUDY CROON: Radio personality who hails from Calgary, Canada.

BILLY CRYSTAL: Director and actor who directed and starred in the film *Forget Paris*. Also star of the film *When Harry Met Sally*. Former cast member of NBC's *Saturday Night Live*. Co-host of HBO's *Comic Relief*.

RODNEY DANGERFIELD: Actor who starred in the films *Caddyshack* and *Back to School*. Most recently appeared in Oliver Stone's film *Natural Born Killers*. He won a Grammy in 1981 for his comedy album *No Respect*.

ELLEN DEGENERES: Star of ABC's *Ellen*. Author of the best-selling *My Point...And I Do Have One*.

PHYLLIS DILLER: Star of 18 movies and author of four books.

JANINE DITULLIO: Writer for *Late Night with Conan O'Brien*.

BECKY DONOHUE: Comedian based in New York City.

WILL DURST: Comedy writer. Nominated for Best Stand-Up Comic–Male at the 1995 American Comedy Awards.

BOB ETTINGER: Appeared on Fox's *Comedy Express*. He has written for Showtime's *The Byron Allen Show*.

SHANG FORBES: Comedian who regularly appears at the Improvisation in Los Angeles.

JEFF FOXWORTHY: Star of ABC's *The Jeff Foxworthy Show*. Best-selling author of the *You Might Be A Redneck If...* series.

JANEANE GAROFALO: Actress who appeared in the film *Reality Bites*. Former co-star of HBO's *The Larry Sanders Show*.

EMMY GAY: Comedian from New York City who performs extensively on the college circuit.

WHOOPI GOLDBERG: Winner of the Best Supporting Actress Oscar for the film *Ghost*. Host of the 68th and 66th annual Academy Awards ceremonies. Co-host of HBO's *Comic Relief*.

BOBCAT GOLDTHWAIT: Actor who has appeared in several films including *Police Academy II*, *Scrooged*, and *Shakes the Clown*, which he also wrote and directed.

MARGA GOMEZ: "Out" comedian who has appeared on *Comic Relief VI*. Creator and star of the performance pieces *Marga Gomez Is Pretty, Witty, and Gay* and *Memory Tricks*.

DICK GREGORY: Comedian and civil rights activist.

JAMES GREGORY: Comedian who appears regularly on The Nashville Network. In 1981 he set a world record for staying on stage 30 continuous hours.

TIM HALPERN: New York-based stand-up comedian who has appeared on MTV.

DARRELL HAMMOND: Cast member of NBC's *Saturday Night Live*.

RHONDA "PASSION" HANSOME: Comedian who has opened for James Brown, the Pointer Sisters, and Anita Baker.

LYNN HARRIS: Stand-up comedian based in New York City. Author of the upcoming book *He Loved Me, He Loves Me Not: A Guide To Fudge, Fury, Free Time, and Life Beyond the Breakup*.

LINDA HERSKOVIC: Appeared in numerous comedy shows including VH-1's *Stand Up Spotlight*.

RICHARD JENI: Actor who appeared in the film *The Mask*. His Showtime special *Richard Jeni 2: Crazy from the Heat* was the highest-rated debut stand-up comedy special for the network.

JAKE JOHANSEN: Host of HBO's *One-Night Stand*. Nominated for Best Stand-Up Comic–Male at the 1995 American Comedy Awards.

JOAN KEITER: Comedian based in New York City.

BARRY KENNEDY: Comedian who used to fly jets for the Canadian Armed Forces.

LAURA KIGHTLINGER: Host of Comedy Central's *Stand Up Stand Up*, and writer for ABC's *Roseanne*. Featured "patient" on Comedy Central's *Dr. Katz, Professional Therapist*.

BRIAN KILEY: Writer for NBC's *Late Night with Conan O'Brien*.

GREG KINNEAR: Actor who co-starred in the 1995 remake of the film *Sabrina*. Host of NBC's *Later with Greg Kinnear*. Former host of E!'s *Talk Soup*.

MARK KLEIN: Published humorist who appeared on A&E's *Comedy on the Road* and Showtime's *Comedy Club Network*.

CATHY LADMAN: Actress and winner of the Best Stand-Up Comic–Female at the 1992 American Comedy Awards.

DENIS LEARY: Writer and star of the film *Two If By Sea*. Star of the one-man show and album *No Cure for Cancer*.

CAROL LEIFER: Co-producer of NBC's *Seinfeld*.

JAY LENO: Host of NBC's *The Tonight Show.*

DAVID LETTERMAN: Host of CBS's *The Late Show.*

RICHARD LEWIS: Co-starred in the former ABC comedy *Anything But Love.* Host of Comedy Central's *The A List.*

WENDY LIEBMAN: Comedian nominated for the Best Stand-Up Comic–Female at the 1995 American Comedy Awards.

RUSH LIMBAUGH: Conservative talk show host, radio personality, and best-selling author of *The Way Things Ought To Be.*

RANDY LUBAS: Appeared on A&E's *Comedy on the Road* and The Nashville Network.

MARLA LUKOFSKY: Appeared on Comedy Central's *Stand Up Stand Up.*

NORM MACDONALD: Cast member of *Saturday Night Live.*

KATHLEEN MADIGAN: Comedian and winner of Best Stand-Up Comic–Female at the 1996 American Comedy Awards.

BILL MAHER: Host of Comedy Central's *Politically Incorrect.*

JACKIE MASON: 30-year comedy veteran. Star of the hit one-man Broadway show *Jackie Mason: Politically Incorrect.*

ETTA MAY: Appeared on ABC's *Hanging with Mr. Cooper.* Also appeared on *The Comedy Store's 15th Anniversary Special.*

KEVIN MCDONALD: Former cast member of Comedy Central's *The Kids in the Hall.*

JOHN MENDOZA: Starred in the former NBC sitcom *The Second Half.*

FELICIA MICHAELS: Played Roxy Martin, a recurring character on ABC's *Full House.* Winner of the 1992 Star Search competition.

BEVERLY MICKINS: Appeared on the former ABC drama *thirtysomething.* Performed at Caroline's Comedy Club and PS 122 in New York.

DENNIS MILLER: Actor and host of HBO's *Dennis Miller Live.* Former cast member of *Saturday Night Live.*

LARRY MILLER: Comedian and featured "patient" on Comedy Central's *Dr. Katz, Professional Therapist.*

ANITA MILNER: Comedian and attorney based in Escondido, California

PAUL MOONEY: Comedian who has been featured on HBO nine times. Writer for Richard Pryor.

ROBIN MONTAGUE: Co-star of the film *Talking Dirty After Dark.* Appeared on HBO's *Def Comedy Jam*

LYNDA MONTGOMERY: "Out" comedian and distant cousin of Alfred Hitchcock

DENISE MUNRO: Profiled on A&E's *Comedy on the Road.*

CONAN O'BRIEN: Host of NBC's *Late Night with Conan O'Brien.* Former writer for Fox's *The Simpsons.*

ROSIE O'DONNELL: Actress, producer, and director who co-starred in the films *Sleepless in Seattle* and *A League of Their Own.*

RICK OVERTON: Appeared in the films *Mrs. Doubtfire* and *Beverly Hills Cop*. Fans of NBC's *Seinfeld* will recognize him as Drake.

MARK PITTA: Host of Fox's *Totally Hidden Videos*. Hosted of the former NBC show *Friday Night Videos*.

PAULA POUNDSTONE: Veteran of numerous HBO appearances.

MICHAEL PRITCHARD: Comedian and former juvenile probation officer. Winner of the San Francisco International Comedy Competition.

RICHARD PRYOR: A 30-year film and television veteran whose comic style has influenced several of today's stars, including Eddie Murphy.

BRIAN REGAN: Winner of Best Stand-Up Comic–Male at the 1996 American Comedy Awards.

PAUL REISER: Star of NBC's *Mad About You*. Author of the best-selling *Couplehood*.

BILLY RIBACK: Writer and producer of ABC's *Home Improvement*.

KAREN RIPLEY: "Out" comedian featured in the video *All Out Comedy*.

JOAN RIVERS: Actress, talk show host, and best-selling author.

GREGG ROGELL: Appeared on CBS's *The Nanny* and NBC's *The Tonight Show*.

ROSEANNE: Star and producer of ABC's *Roseanne*. Co-star of the film *She Devil*. Best-selling author of *My Life as a Woman* and *My Lives*.

RITA RUDNER: Screenwriter and co-star of the film *Peter's Friends*. Author of *Rita Rudner's Guide to Men*. Featured on numerous specials including her own for HBO.

BOB SAGET: Star of ABC's *America's Funniest Home Videos* and of the former ABC sitcom *Full House*.

BETSY SALKIND: Stand-up comedian and filmmaker based in Los Angeles.

ADAM SANDLER: Star of the films *Billy Madison* and *Happy Gilmore*. Former cast member of NBC's *Saturday Night Live*.

JERRY SEINFELD: Star of NBC's *Seinfeld* and author of the best-selling *SeinLanguage*.

GARRY SHANDLING: Star of HBO's *The Larry Sanders Show* and numerous other HBO specials.

PAULY SHORE: Actor and MTV VJ.

SINBAD: Star of the film *House Guest*.

TOMMY SLEDGE: Veteran of numerous comedy shows including Comedy Central's *The A List*. Sometimes known as "The Stand-up Detective."

STUART SMALLEY: A character on NBC's *Saturday Night Live* created by Al Franken–who is also a screenwriter and best-selling author of *Rush Limbaugh Is A Big Fat Idiot*.

BOB SMITH: One of the first "out" comedians to appear on television. Co-author of the book *Growing Up Gay: From Left Out to Coming Out*.

MARGARET SMITH: Appeared on *Bob Hope's 1995 Young Comedians' Special*. Winner of Best Stand-Up Comic–Female at the 1995 American Comedy Awards.

TOMMY SMOTHERS: One half of the comedy team The Smothers Brothers. Starred in the CBS series *The Smothers Brothers* in both the '60s and the '80s.

JON STEWART: Hosted the former MTV show *The Jon Stewart Show*.

JEFF STILSON: Featured in numerous TV shows including the *14th Annual HBO Young Comedians Special*.

JUDY TENUTA: Appeared in her own HBO, Lifetime, and Showtime specials. Author of *The Power of Judyism*. A 1995 Grammy nominee for Comedy Album of the Year.

LILY TOMLIN: Star of several films including *9 to 5*. Original cast member of NBC's *Laugh-In*. Writer, and solo performer who often works in collaboration with the writer/director Jane Wagner.

THEA VIDALE: Star of the former ABC sitcom *Thea*. Appeared in numerous television shows including HBO's *Def Comedy Jam*.

JANE WAGNER: Playwright and author of *The Search for Signs of Intelligent Life in the Universe* starring Lily Tomlin.

GEORGE WALLACE: Comedian and winner of Best Stand-Up Comic–Male at the 1995 American Comedy Awards.

MARSHA WARFIELD: Co-starred in the former NBC sitcom *Night Court*.

SUZANNE WESTENHOEFER: One of the first "out" comedians to have an HBO special.

ROBIN WILLIAMS: Academy Award–nominated star of the films *Mrs. Doubtfire* and *Good Morning, Vietnam*. Star of the former ABC sitcom *Mork and Mindy*. Co-host of HBO's *Comic Relief*.

LIZZ WINSTEAD: Comedian who will be appearing in *Setting the Agenda: Indecision '96*, a new special shot at the U.S. Comedy Arts Festival in Aspen. She is currently developing a new series for Comedy Central called *The Network*.

ANITA WISE: Appeared on NBC's *Seinfeld* and A&E's *Evening at the Improv*.

STEVEN WRIGHT: Television actor who was recently nominated for an Oscar for best short film.

ROBERT WUHL: Appeared in the films *Batman*, *Cobb*, and *Good Morning, Vietnam*. Star of his own HBO Comedy Hour, *Robert Wuhl's World Tour*.

HENNY YOUNGMAN: A 50-year comedy veteran best known for his one-liners like, "Take my wife...please."

The Comedy Directory

ALABAMA

Comedy Club
–Huntsville
Hilton Hotel Downtown
401 Williams Street
Huntsville, AL 35801
(205) 536-3329

The Comedy Club at
the Stardome
1818 Data Drive
Birmingham, AL 35244
(205) 444-0008

ALASKA

Pierce Street Annex
301 East Tudor Road
Anchorage, AK 99503
(907) 563-5633

ARIZONA

Improv
930 University Dr. &
Rural Rd.
Suite D1-201
Tempe, AZ 85281
(602) 921-9877

Three Jokers
2020 N. Arizona Ave.
Chandler, AZ 85244
(602) 786-1800

ARKANSAS

Stanford's Comedy
House
Rodney Parham Road

Little Rock, AR
(501) 228-5555

CALIFORNIA

Catalina Comedy Club
116 Summer
Avalon, CA 90704
(310) 510-1400

Cobb's Comedy Club
2801 Leavenworth
San Francisco, CA
94133
(415) 928-4320

Comedy Act Theatre
3339 West 43rd Street
Los Angeles, CA 90008
(310) 677-4101

The Comedy Club
Hornblowers
1559 Spinnaker Drive
Ventura, CA 93001
(310) 275-3658

Comedy & Magic Club
1018 Hermosa Avenue
Hermosa Beach, CA
90254
(310) 376-6914

Comedy Isle
Bahia Hotel
998 W. Mission Bay Dr.
San Diego, CA 92109
(619) 488-6872

Comedy Store–La Jolla
916 Pearl Street
La Jolla, CA 92037
(619) 454-9178

Ice House
24 N. Mentor Ave.
Pasadena, CA 91106
(818) 577-1894

Igby's
11637 Pico Blvd.
W. Los Angeles, CA
90064
(310) 477-3553

Improv–Brea
945 East Birch Street
Brea, CA 92621
(714) 529-7878

Improv–Hollywood
8162 Melrose Avenue
Hollywood, CA 90046
(213) 651-2583

Knuckleheads
645 Downtown Plaza
Sacramento, CA 95128
(916) 447-4700

Knuckleheads
150 South First Street
#237
San Jose, CA 95113
(408) 291-2231

L.A. Cabaret Comedy
Club
17271 Ventura Blvd.
Encino, CA 91316
(818) 501-3737

L.A. Connection
Comedy Theatre
13442 Ventura Blvd.
Sherman Oaks, CA
91428
(818) 748-1868

Laugh Factory
8001 Sunset Blvd.
West Hollywood, CA
90046
(213) 656-1336

Laughs Unlimited
1207 Front Street
Old Sacramento, CA
95814
(916) 446-5905

Planet Gemini
625 Cannery Row
Monterey, CA 93940
(408) 373-1617

Punchline
2100 Arden Way
Sacramento, CA 95825
(916) 925-5500

Punchline
444 Battery Street
San Francisco, CA
94111
(415) 397-4337

Rooster T. Feathers
157 W. El Camino Real
Sunnyvale, CA 94806
(408) 736-0921

Screwballs
1231 Van Ness Blvd.
Fresno, CA 93721
(209) 268-0258

Sunshine Saloon
1807 Santa Rita Road
Suite K
Pleasanton, CA 95466
(510) 846-6108

COLORADO

The Comedy Club
10015-A East Hampden
Avenue

Denver, CO 80231
(303) 368-8900

Comedy Works
1226 15th Street
Denver, CO 80202
(303) 595-3637

Laff's Comedy Corner
1305 N. Academy Blvd.
Colorado Springs, CO
80909
(719) 591-0707

CONNECTICUT

The Bombay
Bicycle Club
1360 Silas Dean Hgwy
Rocky Hill, CT 06067
(203) 563-6517

Treehouse–Mystic
Best Western Hotel
158 Greenville Road
Mystic, CT 06355
(203) 536-7126

Treehouse–Norwalk
50 Isaac Street
Norwalk, CT 06850
(203) 838-2424

Treehouse–Southbury
Longhorn's Restaurant
57 Oak Street Road
Southbury, CT 06488
(203) 264-4343

DELAWARE

Comedy Cabaret
Willowby's Restaurant
1001 Jefferson St. Plaza
Wilmington, DE 19801
(302) 652-6873

DISTRICT OF COLUMBIA

Improv–D.C.
1140 Connecticut Ave.
NW
Washington, D.C.
20036
(202) 296-6988

FLORIDA

Bonkers
120 North Orange Ave.
Orlando, FL
(407) 629-2665

Coconuts
Adams Mark
Caribbean Golf Resort
30 S. Gulf View Blvd.
Clearwater Beach, FL
34630
(813) 443-5714

Coconuts
Quality Inn
St. Petersburg Beach,
FL 33706
(813) 360-JOKE

Coconuts–Lakeland
3311 US Highway 98 N.
Lakeland, FL 33805
(813) 687-2678

Coconuts–Pensacola
Holiday Inn
University Mall/
7200 Plantation Rd.
Pensacola, FL
(904) 484-6887

Coconuts–Sarasota
Ramada Inn Airport
8440 Tamiani Trail
Sarasota, FL 34243
(813) 335-7771

Comedy Corner
2000 S. Dixie Highway
West Palm Beach, FL
  33401
(407) 833-1812

Comedy House
  Theater–Ocala
Holiday Inn
3621 West Silver
  Springs Blvd
Ocala, FL 32675
(904) 732-2665

Comedy Zone–
  Jacksonville
Ramada Inn Mandarin
3130 Hartley Road
Jacksonville, FL 32257

Comedy Zone–
  Tallahassee
Ramada Inn
2900 North Monroe St.
Tallahassee, FL 32303
(904) 386-1027

Comedy Zone–
  Winter Park
Holiday Inn
626 Lee Road
Winter Park, FL 32810
(407) 645-5600

Groucho's
Nassau Center
Nassau Blvd.
Melbourne, FL 32901
(407)724-1220

McCurdy's
Best Western
455 U.S. 41 Bypass N.
Venice, FL 34292
(941) 4855-411

Improv
Bleechers Sports Bar
10478 Roosevelt Blvd.
St. Petersburg, FL
  33716
(813) 578-0232

McCurdy's Comedy
  Club
Holiday Inn Airport
7150 N. Tamiami Trail
Sarasota, FL 34243
(813) 355-2781

Sanibel Island Comedy
  Club
975 Rabbit Road
Sanibel Island, FL
  33957
(941) 472-8833

Sidesplitters
12938 North Dale
  Mabry Highway
Tampa, FL 33618
(813) 960-1197

Uncle Funny's Comedy
  Niteclub
9160 State Road 84
Davie, FL 33324
(305) 474-5653

GEORGIA

Punchline–Atlanta
280 Hilderbrand Drive
Atlanta, GA 30328
(404) 252-5233

Uptown Comedy
  Corner
2140 Peachtree Road
Atlanta, GA 30309
(404) 350-6990

HAWAII

Honolulu Comedy Club
Astin Waikiki Terrace
  Hotel
2045 Kalakaula Ave.
Honolulu, HI 96815
(808) 922-59998

ILLINOIS

All Jokes Aside
1000 South Wabash St.
Chicago, IL 60605
(312) 922-0577

Barrel of Laughs
10345 S. Central Ave.
Oaklawn, IL 60453
(708) 499-2969

Comedy Etc.
6900 North Illinois
I-64 and Illinois-159
Fairview Heights, IL
  62208
(618) 628-4242

ComedySportz–Rock
  Island
The Speakeasy
1828 Third Avenue
Rock Island, IL 61201
(309) 786-2667

Fun Seekers
684 West North Ave.
Elmhurst, IL 60126
(708) 993-0423

Funnybone–Naperville
1504 N. Naper Blvd.
Naperville, IL 60563
(708) 995-0500

Jukebox Comedy Club
and Lounge, Inc.
3527 W. Farmington
Peoria, IL 61604
(309) 673-5853

K.J. Riddles
15750 South Harlem
Orlando Park, IL 60463
(708) 614-6336

T.N.T. Comedy Hook
2352 East 172nd Street
Lansing, IL 60430
(708) 418-1700

Zanies–Mt. Prospect
2200 S. Elmhurst Rd.
Mt. Prospect, IL 60056
(708) 228-6166

Zanies–Pheasant Run
Pheasant Run Resort
4051 East Main Street
St. Charles IL 60174
(708) 513-1761

Zanies-Vernon Hills
230 Hawthorne Village
Commons
Vernon Hills, IL 60061
(708) 549-6030

INDIANA

Broad Ripple Comedy
Club
6281 N. College Ave.
Indianapolis, IN 46220
(317) 255-4211

Crackers Comedy Club
8702 Keystone
Crossing
Indianapolis, IN 46240
(317) 846-2500

Funny Bones–Indiana
1290 Scottsdale Mall

South Bend, IN 46612
(219)299-9999

Indianapolis Comedy
Connection
247 S. Meridian St.
Indianapolis, IN 46225
(317) 631-3536

Snickerz Comedy Bar
5535 St. Joe Road
Fort Wayne, IN 46835
(219) 486-0216

Wisecrackers
Radison Hotel at Star
Plaza
800 East 81st Avenue
Merryville, IN 46410
(219) 769-6311

IOWA

Funny Bones–Des
Moines
Cobblestone Market
8529 Hickman
Urbandale, IA 50322
(515) 270-2100

Penguin's Comedy Club
209 First Avenue SE
Cedar Rapids, IA 52401
(319) 362-8133

Pepperoni's Comedy
Club
Alfredo Pizza
523 West 19th Street
Sioux City, IA 51103
(712) 258-0691

KENTUCKY

Comedy Caravan
Mid City Mall
1250 Bardstown Road
Louisville, KY 40299
(502) 459-0022

LOUISIANA

Funnybone-Baton
Rouge
4715 Bennington
Baton Rouge, LA 70808
(504) 928-9996

MAINE

Comedy Connection
6 Custom House Wharf
Portland, ME 04101
(207) 774-5554

MARYLAND

Big Mike's Cafe
Holiday Inn at
Aberdeen/Rt. 22
Havre de Grace, MD
21078
(410) 939-2877

Comedy Connection
312 Main Street
Laurel, MD 20707
(301) 490-1993

New York Comedy Club
Giovanni's Restaurant
3301 Coastal Highway
Ocean City, MD 21811
(410) 289-4588
(Opening 5/96)

MASSACHUSETTS

Comedy Cafe
Holiday Inn
1374 North Main Street
Randolph, MA 02368
(617) 961-1000

Comedy Connection
Quincy Market Bldg.
Faneuil Marketplace
Boston, MA 02109
(617) 248-9700

Comedy Palace
Grill 93 at River Road
Andover, MA 01810
(508) 682-9464

Dick Doherty's
Comedy Hut II
Aku-Aku Restaurant
11 East Central Street
Worcester, MA 06108
(508) 792-1126

Dick Doherty's
Comedy Vault
Remmington's of
Boston
124 Boylston Street
Boston, MA 021176
(617) 574-9676

Giggles Comedy Club
Prince Restaurant
517 Broadway
Saugus, MA 01906
(617) 233-9950

Nick's
Kowloon Restaurant
Rt. 1 North
Saugus, MA 02906
(617) 231-2500

Nick's at Maui
1875 Main Street
Brockton, MA 02401
(508) 583-1010

Nick's Comedy Stop
100 Warrenton Street
Boston, MA 02116
(617) 482-0930

MICHIGAN

All Jokes Aside of
Detroit
2036 Woodward Ave.
Detroit, MI 48201
(313) 962-2100

Chaplain's–East
Groesbeck Highway
Clinton Township, MI
48035
(810) 792-1902

Chaplain's–West
16890 Telegraph Rd.
Detroit, MI 48219
(313) 533-8866

Comedy Castle
269 East Fourth Street
Royal Oak, MI 48067
(810) 542-9900

Comedy Den
2845 Thorn Hills SE
Grand Rapids, MI
49546
(616) 949-9322

Connxtions Comedy
Club
2900 NE Street
Lansing, MI 48906
(517) 482-1468

Gary Field's Comedy
Club
2580 Capitol Ave. SW
Battle Creek, MI 49015
(616) 965-4646

Main Street Comedy
Showcase
314 East Liberty
Ann Arbor, MI 48104
(313) 996-9080

MINNESOTA

Acme Comedy Co.
708 First Street North
Minneapolis, MN
55401
(612) 338-6393

Knuckleheads–MN
Mall of America

Bloomington, MN
55425
(612) 854-5233

MISSISSIPPI

Comedy Zone
Sheraton Casino
1107 Casino Center Dr.
Robinsonville, MS
38664
(601) 363-4900

MISSOURI

Funnybone–South
County
19 Ronnie's Plaza
St. Louis, MO 63126
(314) 843-2727

Stanford's Comedy
House
5028 Main Street
Kansas City, MO
(816) 756-1450
(Opening 5/96)

NEVADA

Comedy Stop at the
Tropicana
3801 Las Vegas Blvd. S.
Las Vegas, NV 89109
(702) 739-2714

The Hilton
2500 East Second St.
Reno, NV 89595
(702) 789-2078

Riviera Comedy Club
Riviera Hotel
2901 Las Vegas Blvd.
South
Las Vegas, NV 89109
(702) 794-9207

NEW JERSEY

Catch A Rising Star
Hyatt Regency
Route 1
Princeton, NJ
(609) 987-1234

Rascal's–West Orange
425 Pleasant Valley
  Way
West Orange, NJ 07052
(201) 736-2726

NEW MEXICO

Laff's Comedy Caffe
3100-D Juan Tabo Blvd.
  NE
Albuquerque, NM
  87111
(505) 296-5653

NEW YORK

Banana's
Best Western Hotel
679 Route 9
Poughkeepsie, NY
  12601
(914) 462-3333

Boston Comedy
  Club
82 West Third Street
New York, NY 10012
(212) 477-1000

Caroline's
1626 Broadway
New York, NY 10019
(212) 757-4100

Comedy Cellar
107 MacDougal Street
New York, NY 10012
(212) 354-3480

Comic Strip
1568 Second Avenue
New York, NY 10028
(212) 861-9386

Funnybone
880 Alberta Drive
Amherst, NY 14226
(716) 838-2800

Grampa's Comedy
  Club
106 New Dorp Plaza
Staten Island, NY
  10306
(718) 667-4242

New York Comedy
  Club
241 East 24th Street
New York, NY 10010
(212) 696-5233

Pips
2005 Emmons Ave.
Brooklyn, NY
(718) 646-9433

NORTH CAROLINA

Charlie Goodnight's
861 W. Morgan Street
Raleigh, NC 27605
(919) 833-3707

The Comedy Club
The Carolinian Hotel
Nagshead, NC 27959
(919) 441-7171

OHIO

Hilarities
1230 West 6th Street
Cleveland, OH
(216) 443-1077

The Improvisation
2000 Sycamore #1

Cleveland, OH
(216) 696-4677

The Funny Bone
6312 Busch Blvd.
Columbus, OH 43229
(614) 431-1471

OREGON

Harvey's Comedy Club
  and Restaurant
436 NW Sixth Street
Portland, OR 97209
(503) 241-0338

PENNSYLVANIA

Comedy Cabaret
625 North Main Street
Doylestown, PA 18190
(215) 345-5653

Comedy Cabaret
Middle East Restaurant
126 Chestnut Street
Philadelphia, PA 19106
(215) 625-5653

Funnybone
The Shops at Station
  Square
Pittsburgh, PA 15219
(412) 281-3130

Villa East Comedy
2331 Lincoln Hwy East
Lancaster, PA 17602
(717) 397-4973

SOUTH CAROLINA

Coconuts
15 Heritage Plaza
Hilton Head, SC 29928
(803) 686-6887

SOUTH DAKOTA

Philly's Comedy
Shoppe
Rapid City Inn
445 Mt. Rushmore Rd.
Rapid City, SD 57701
(605) 348-8300

TENNESSEE

Comedy Zone
2125 Madison Avenue
Memphis, TN 38104
(901) 278-7861

Zanies
2025 Eighth Ave.
South
Nashville, TN 37204
(615) 269-0221

TEXAS

Comedy Showcase
12547 Gulf Freeway at
Fuqua
Houston, TX 77034
(713) 481-1188

Esther's Follies
525 East Sixth Street
Austin, TX 78701
(512) 320-553

High Tide Comedy
Marriott Hotel
900 N. Shoreline Blvd.
Corpus Christi, TX
78401

Capitol City Comedy
Club
8120 Research Blvd.
Austin, TX 78758
(512) 467-2333

Laff Stop
1952A West Gray
Houston, TX 77019
(713) 524-2333

River Center Comedy
Club
849 East Commerce
#893
San Antonio, TX 78205
(210) 229-1420

Velveeta Room
521 East Sixth Street
Austin, TX 78701
(512) 469-9116

UTAH

The Comedy Circuit
7720 South 700 West
Midvale, UT 84047
(801) 561-7777

Johnny B's
177 West 300 South
Provo, UT 84601
(801) 377-6910

VERMONT

Comedy Zone
Radisson Hotel
60 Battery Street
Burlington, VT 05401
(802) 658-6500

VIRGINIA

Cozzy's Comedy Club
and Tavern
9700 Warwick Blvd,
Newport News, VA
23601
(804) 595-2800

Roanoke Comedy Club
632 Townside Road
Roanoke, VA 24011
(504) 982-5693

Thoroughgood Inn
Comedy Club
4520 Pembroke
Meadows Center
Virginia Beach, VA
23455
(804) 499-7071

WASHINGTON

Comedy Underground
222 South Main Street
Seattle, WA 98104
(206) 622-4550

WEST VIRGINIA

Comedy Zone
Holiday Inn
1000 Washington St.
Charleston, WV 25302
(304) 343-4661

WISCONSIN

Comedy Cafe
615 East Brady Street
Milwaukee, WI 53202
(414) 271-5653

ComedySportz
PO Box 5102
Madison, WI 53705
(608) 255-8888

Comedy Showcase

AMERICAN DREAM
  FESTIVAL
7314 San Sebastian Dr.
Boca Raton, Florida
  33433
(407) 391-0789

KÖLN COMEDY FESTIVAL
Martin-Luther Platz 13
50677 Köln, Germany
011 49 0221-3750
011 49 0221-3427

LUCILLE BALL FESTIVAL
  OF NEW COMEDY
116 East Third Street
Jamestown, NY
(716) 664-2465
(716) 664-3829 FAX

MELBOURNE COMEDY
  FESTIVAL
P.O. Box 341 Fitzroy
  3065

Melbourne, Australia
011 61 3 417-7711
011 61 3 417-5540 FAX

MONTREAL'S JUST FOR
  LAUGHS INTERNATIONAL
  COMEDY FESTIVAL
51 Sherbrooke West
Montreal, Quebec,
Canada
H2X 1X2
(514) 845-3155
(514) 845-4140 FAX

THE PEOPLE'S COMEDY
  FESTIVAL
c/o Yuk Yuk's Int'l
1280 Bay Street/Upper
Concourse
Toronto, Ontario
Canada MSR 3L1
(416) 967-6341
(416) 925-9298 FAX

TOYOTA COMEDY
  FESTIVAL
c/o Festival
  Productions
311 West 74th Street
New York, NY 10023
(212) 496-9000

VAIL NATIONAL COMEDY
  INVITATIONAL
NSD Productions
4470 Sunset Blvd.
Los Angeles, California
  90027
(213) 660-6656
(213) 662-4283 FAX